THE SHEPHERD'S VOICE

A JOURNEY OF DISCERNMENT IN A NOISY WORLD

Tonnines Elliott

 *Published by* So It Is Written, LLC
Rochester, MI
SoItIsWritten.net

The Shepherd's Voice: A Journey of Discernment in a Noisy World
Copyright © 2026 by Tonnines Elliott

All rights reserved. No part of this book may be reproduced or transmitted in any form or by any means, electronic or mechanical, including photocopying, recording, or by an information storage and retrieval system—except by a reviewer who may quote brief passages in a review to be printed in a magazine or newspaper—without permission in writing from the publisher.

All rights reserved. No part of this book may be reproduced or transmitted in any form or by any means— electronic, mechanical, photocopying, recording, or otherwise—without prior written permission of the author, except in the case of brief quotations used in reviews or articles.

Scripture quotations are taken from the New King James Version®. Copyright © 1982 by Thomas Nelson. Used by permission. All rights reserved.

Scripture quotations are taken from the Holy Bible, New International Version®. Copyright © 1973, 1978, 1984, 2011 by Biblica, Inc.® Used by permission. All rights reserved worldwide.

Scripture quotations are from The Message. Copyright © by Eugene H. Peterson. All rights reserved. Used by permission of NavPress.

Edited by: So It Is Written – www.SoItIsWritten.net

Cover design by: Tonnines Elliott

Formatting: Ya Ya Ya Creative – YaYaYaCreative@gmail.com

ISBN: 979-8-9945584-0-9
LCCN: 2026901917

PRINTED AND BOUND IN THE UNITED STATES OF AMERICA

TABLE OF CONTENTS

Prelude–THE VOICE ON THE WIND 1

THE MASK AND THE MESSAGE 5

MESSAGE TO THE READER 13

PART 1: FOUNDATIONS OF DISCERNMENT 15
Chapter 1–THE FORK IN THE ROAD 17

Chapter 2–THE ANATOMY OF MANIPULATION 23

Chapter 3–THE WOLF IN SHEPHERD'S CLOTHING . . 29

Chapter 4–THE BIBLICAL FOUNDATION
OF DISCERNMENT 37

PART 2: EVERYDAY RESPONSES 43
Chapter 5–"IT'S JUST A DIFFERENCE OF OPINION" . 45

Chapter 6–THE FRUITS OF MANIPULATION 51

Chapter 7–THE COST OF SILENCE 57

**PART 3: THE CULTURAL CHALLENGE
OF NATIONALISM** 63
Chapter 8–THE UNSETTLING FUSION 65

Chapter 9–WHAT IS WHITE CHRISTIAN NATIONALISM? 71

Chapter 10–WHAT IS RIGHT-WING CHRISTIAN
NATIONALISM? 81

Chapter 11–THE SEDUCTION OF NATIONALISM 93

Chapter 12–RESTORING THE WITNESS 103

Chapter 13–THE HISTORICAL CONSEQUENCES OF
NATIONALISM IN THE CHURCH 113

Chapter 14–THE FRUITS OF NATIONALISM IN THE
CHURCH TODAY 119

PART 4: THE WAY FORWARD 125
Chapter 15–THE BIBLICAL RESPONSE
TO NATIONALISM 127

Chapter 16–PRACTICAL TOOLS FOR DISCERNMENT
IN DAILY LIFE 135

CONCLUSION 141

APPENDICES INTRODUCTION 145

Appendix A–SCRIPTURE REFERENCES 147

Appendix B–REFLECTION & DISCUSSION GUIDE . . 157

Appendix C–KEY TERMS & DEFINITIONS 175

REFERENCES 177

ABOUT THE AUTHOR 181

PRELUDE

THE VOICE ON THE WIND

On a Sunday afternoon that smelled like rain and cut grass, Marcus Hale scrolled his phone in the back row of his church. The worship team had just finished a chorus he used to love—something about still waters and a Shepherd's call—but his thumb kept moving, flicking up short clips stitched together by an algorithm he trusted more than he realized. The sanctuary lights glowed warm against the stained glass, and dust hung in the air like a quiet snowfall. A few rows ahead, a child whispered the last word of each lyric a beat behind everyone else, trying to keep up. The air conditioner hummed, the ushers moved softly, the amens were steady—familiar as the pew he'd known since his twenties. Yet beneath that familiarity, a restlessness tugged at him, the way an unsettled wind lifts the edge of a page.

Titles flashed like warning lights: *Truth they don't want you to hear. Saving the nation for Christ. Why genuine believers must take a stand.* Commenters cheered. He nodded along, feeling a fire that called itself courage.

If you'd asked Marcus two years earlier, he would have said he was just a husband, a dad, a small business owner. He coached Little League. He served on the tech team, where he learned to fade lights and clean audio, so sermons felt clear and steady. Outside of Sunday mornings, life moved in dependable circles—school pickups, invoices, practice schedules, the familiar madness of a grocery run on a Saturday. He wasn't a "political guy," he told friends. Just "concerned." Concern had become a habit. Concern became a playlist. And the playlist became a path.

The Strategy of the Algorithm

It started small. A new "Christian" streaming show with clean branding and a host who quoted a verse here, a statistic there. He spoke of "heritage," "order," and "the way things used to be." It was nostalgia lacquered with Bible words. The host said the Church needed to "wake up." Marcus liked the sound of that. He followed. He shared. His feed obliged, serving more of the same.

The voices grew louder—more certain, more edged—though the graphics stayed clean, the language stayed "godly," and the verses—stripped from their paragraphs—landed like gavel strikes. The urgency felt spiritual; the cadence mimicked conviction. Each episode promised a kind of clarity that made complex people look simple and made difficult questions feel like disloyalty. The more he

PRELUDE—*The Voice on the Wind*

watched, the more he mistook agitation for discernment, adrenaline for faith.

Eli noticed first. He always did. They had been friends since their sons were toddlers, back when summer nights were spent on sprinklers in the yard and collecting lightning bugs in jars with holes punched into the lids. Eli was the soft-spoken one in their men's group. He was the first to volunteer for a meal train and the last to post on social media. He'd show up to help you move a couch and leave before you had time to say thank you. When he texted, "Coffee this week?" Marcus said yes without thinking.

At the diner, Eli cupped his hands around a chipped mug and watched the steam rise. He didn't begin with a lecture; he began with a question. "How are you—really?" The word hung between them with room to answer and room to hide.

"I'm fine," Marcus said, too quickly. "Just paying attention. Someone has to."

Eli nodded, like he'd expected that answer and loved him anyway. "I've been praying for you," he said gently. "Just… test what you're hearing. Jesus said, 'We know trees by their fruit.'" He slid his phone across the table with Galatians 5 on the screen: "The fruit of the Spirit is love, joy, peace, forbearance, kindness, goodness, faithfulness, gentleness and self-control."

He tapped the list, then looked up. "When you finish a show, does your spirit feel like this—or like fear and contempt?"

Marcus felt the question more than he heard it. He deflected. "Finally, somebody's standing up for truth. For our people." The last two words surprised him as they left his mouth. *Our people.*

Eli didn't argue. He let the silence do a little work, then smiled and changed the subject. Later, when they stood to go, he left a sticky note under the sugar caddy with a verse he'd already shown him—just in case. "Love, joy, peace…" The note would find its way beneath Marcus's truck visor by evening.

THE MASK AND
THE MESSAGE

Over the next couple of months, the show taught Marcus a new vocabulary: wolves, traitors, real Christians, just war, our culture, and their takeover. He joined a group chat that curated "receipts" of supposed enemies—pastors, neighbors, scholars, immigrants, anyone who questioned the host's claims. Bible verses captioned memes; memes became doctrine. A guest speaker explained that loving the nation was equivalent to loving God. Another insisted that to question their strategy was to "side with evil." It sounded brave. It felt like purpose.

The more certain the host became, the more suspicious Marcus felt toward anyone who asked him to slow down. When his pastor preached on loving God and loving neighbor, the message felt off-key, almost naïve. On the drive home, he said, "Love is soft." He didn't mean to say it out loud. His daughter stared at her hands in her lap and asked softly, "Dad, who counts as an invader?"

He didn't have an answer he liked. He changed the subject and turned up the radio.

Eli kept dropping by, sometimes just to return a borrowed drill, sometimes with a dozen of his wife's cookies, wrapped in wax paper. He never cornered, never scolded. A verse would appear on a sticky note by the sink, on the garage workbench, tucked beneath a magnet on the fridge: "There is neither Jew nor Gentile… for you are all one in Christ Jesus." Or: "God does not show favoritism but accepts from every nation the one who fears Him and does what is right." Marcus didn't throw them away, but he learned to look past them, as if Scripture could be set to the edge of a workbench until there was time for it later.

The Night of the Sirens

Summer crept in, and with it the rally: a "night of prayer and action" downtown. The stage washed gold across a sea of flags. Marcus took a sign from a volunteer and found a spot near the middle where he could see and be seen. The opening song was familiar—a chorus from his childhood. He sang the first verse with a lump in his throat, not knowing whether to call it zeal or nostalgia.

The host took the platform, flanked by men in tactical vests. The speech began with Jesus and then shifted to "heritage." It ended with a warning: "Don't let them take what God gave you." Across the street, candles flickered in the hands of another group, their hymn quiet and steady. The man on the platform mocked their softness. A jeer. A shove. A bottle arced, then shattered. It wasn't clear who threw it. Sirens wailed. People ran. A young woman cried out, "I'm hit!" and fell.

Marcus felt the sound more than he heard it. He crouched near the curb as strangers held their hands up, palms shaking. The host slipped through a back exit. The flags snapped in the wind.

He stood very still, as if stillness could reverse the moment. Across the street, a man kept singing the last line of the hymn after everyone else had stopped, voice thin and faithful. Marcus stared at him for a long time, as if the answer to a question he hadn't asked might be spelled on that man's mouth.

The Wolf's Cloak

At 1 a.m., the house was nearly silent. The dryer ticked as it cooled. Rain returned and softened the dark. Marcus poured coffee and opened his Bible without a plan, the way you open a window for air. It fell to Proverbs 6: "There are six things the Lord hates... a lying tongue, a heart that devises wicked plans... a false witness... one who sows discord among brothers." The words landed with an uncomfortable specificity. He flipped to Matthew 7: "Watch out for false prophets. They come to you in sheep's clothing, but inwardly they are ferocious wolves… By their fruit you will recognize them."

He pictured the rally, the chant that felt like courage, the laughter that sounded like scorn, the thin hymn across the street. He heard Eli's question again: "When you finish, does your spirit feel like love, joy, peace… or like fear and contempt?"

For the first time in months, he didn't post. He didn't forward a clip. He put the phone face down and let the rain fill the room like a prayer he didn't know how to pray.

"What fruit am I eating? What fruit am I bearing?" he whispered to a God he had not stopped loving, but whom he had been trying to lead.

The Messenger

"Can we talk?" he texted Eli at dawn.

They met under a live oak in the park after work, when the heat had lifted and the shadows grew a soft edge. Two boys rode bicycles in crooked circles near the bench. Somewhere a lawn mower droned, stopping and starting in clumps of sound. Marcus spoke first, halting and then steady, about the rally, about the scream, about the verses that cut through his sleep.

Eli listened with the patience of a man who believes God is already at work long before he sees proof. When Marcus finished, Eli nodded, as if they were agreeing on something ancient and kind. "Brother," he said, "I've been praying you'd hear the Shepherd's voice again. Not the show's version. His."

He opened to John 10 and read softly: "My sheep hear My voice; I know them, and they follow Me… The thief comes only to steal and kill and destroy; I came that they may have life." He let the words rest between them. "Discernment isn't suspicion," he said at last. "It's peace that knows the difference between a shepherd and a salesman."

They prayed on the bench, two men in a public park, heads bowed like boys. Marcus confessed the contempt he had called conviction, the pride he had called faith, the hunger to belong that had dressed itself up as courage. When they said 'amen,' the wind moved through the oak leaves like a breath.

Repentance in the Public Square

Back home, Marcus unfollowed the host. He left the chat. He scrolled through old messages and sent three apologies—to a brother-in-law he'd argued with, to a neighbor he'd mocked behind his back, to a friend from church he'd treated like a suspect. He didn't try to explain; he confessed.

On Sunday, he asked for five minutes after service and stood behind the microphone he had tuned for others a hundred times. The sanctuary looked the same as it always had—the scratches on the baptistry rail, the corner pew where Mrs. Robinson fanned herself in July, the cross he had dusted on Maundy Thursday. He felt the steadiness of it like a hand on his shoulder.

"If I've wounded you with my words," he said, "I'm sorry. I confused anger with zeal and suspicion with discernment. I forgot that the fruit of the Spirit tastes like love and peace, not rage. Jesus is teaching me again to hear His voice." No one applauded. They didn't need to. A hush moved through the room the way peace sometimes does, quietly, like something returning home.

Eli smiled the way a prayer smiles when it's answered.

The Cost and the Calling

A few months later, Marcus helped start a group for people recovering from spiritual manipulation. He told his story honestly. He told how he fell, what God restored, and how Scripture became his compass again.

He also told them how to test a teacher: By the fruit of the Spirit (Galatians 5:22–23); by the commandment to love (Matthew 22:37–39); by the unity of believers (Galatians 3:28); by God's impartial welcome (Acts 10:34–35); and by the warning of wolves (Matthew 7:15–16).

He ended each meeting the same way: "The Shepherd's voice is not the loudest in the square, but it is the one that leads home."

A Word to the Reader

If you find yourself somewhere on Marcus's path, already in the echo chamber or just starting down the road, hear this with love: God is not embarrassed by your confusion, and He is not powerless before your fear. He is a Shepherd who still speaks.

If you are a friend like Eli—patient, prayerful, or sometimes ignored—be encouraged. Truth spoken in love is never wasted. Repentance isn't a defeat; it's the doorway back to peace.

The Shepherd's voice is calling. Listen and live. *"My sheep hear My voice; I know them, and they follow Me"* (John 10:27).

MESSAGE TO THE READER

As you read these words, I want you to know this book was written with you in mind. My hope is not to point fingers or stir up arguments, but to walk alongside you as we navigate what it means to live faithfully in a noisy and divided world.

Many of us have experienced what people call "church hurt." Sadly, when the fruit of the Spirit is absent, it leaves deep wounds. Maybe you've been ostracized, criticized, or made to feel less-than by those who claimed to speak for Christ. If that's you, I want you to know you are seen, you are loved, and your pain is real.

Galatians 5:22–23 says, "But the fruit of the Spirit is love, joy, peace, forbearance, kindness, goodness, faithfulness, gentleness and self-control." Where manipulation, rivalry or bitterness show up instead, a spirit that is not of Christ is revealed. James 3:16 reminds us: "For where you have envy and selfish ambition, there you find disorder and every evil practice."

The kind of rhetoric that turns on a brother or sister in Christ or labels them an enemy simply for asking questions is not the gospel. If love is missing, something has gone terribly wrong.

Jesus said, "By this everyone will know that you are my disciples, if you love one another" (John 13:35).

I don't know what brought you to this book. Perhaps curiosity, perhaps frustration, perhaps hope. Whatever the reason, my prayer is that you'll find encouragement here. Not all who claim Christ reflect His Spirit perfectly—none of us do—but His voice can still be heard. He still calls, still guides, and still heals.

May these pages remind you that you are not alone, and that God's truth and love are far greater than the noise around us.

PART 1

FOUNDATIONS OF DISCERNMENT

CHAPTER 1

THE FORK IN THE ROAD
Two Paths of Communication

The Power of Communication

Words shape worlds. From the very beginning of Scripture, creation itself is born from communication: "And God said, 'Let there be light,' and there was light" (Genesis 1:3). Communication is never neutral. It carries the power to build or destroy, to bring clarity or confusion, to nurture life or sow death.

Every interaction we have is a fork in the road. We either walk down the path of truth, honesty, and love, or down the path of manipulation, distortion, and control.

Good Communication: Building Bridges

Healthy communication reflects God's character. It is rooted in:

- **Clarity** – speaking so others can understand (Colossians 4:6)
- **Honesty** – telling the truth even when it costs (Ephesians 4:25)

- **Love** – speaking for the good of the other, not just ourselves (1 Corinthians 13:1)
- **Listening** – honoring others by valuing their voice (James 1:19)

When practiced in this way, communication builds trust, strengthens relationships, and draws people closer together.

Corrupted Communication: Breaking Trust

Communication can also be twisted. Just as Satan deceived Eve in the garden with words, communication can be used to manipulate, confuse, or dominate.

Signs of destructive communication include:

- **Deception** – bending the truth for personal gain.
- **Gaslighting** – making others question their memory or sanity.
- **Weaponized silence** – withholding words to punish or control.
- **Fear-based messaging** – shaping behavior through threats or intimidation.

The Fork in the Road

At every moment, we stand at a fork in the road. Which voice will we follow? The voice of truth that leads to freedom, or the voice of manipulation that leads to bondage?

Jesus warned in John 10:10 NIV, "The thief comes only to steal and kill and destroy; I have come that they may have life, and have it to the full."

Our words either align with the Good Shepherd who brings life or with the enemy who twists communication to harm.

Why This Foundation Matters

Before we can discern manipulation, we must first understand the role of communication itself. Recognizing the difference between healthy and unhealthy communication sets the stage for everything else in this book.

Discernment begins not with suspicion, but with noticing whether words bring clarity and life, or confusion and fear.

Reflection Questions

- When you think of communication in your own life, do you more often experience it as life-giving or draining? Why?

  _____

  _____

  _____

- Can you remember a time when someone's honest and loving communication built you up? How did it impact you?

  _____

  _____

  _____

- What are some examples you've seen of destructive communication (in family, church, workplace)? How did it affect trust?

  _____

  _____

  _____

CHAPTER 1—*Reflection Questions*

- How can you become more attentive to the "fork in the road" moments in your daily conversations?

  _____

  _____

  _____

- What practical step can you take this week to make your communication reflect the clarity, honesty, and love of Christ?

  _____

  _____

  _____

CHAPTER 2

THE ANATOMY OF MANIPULATION

Manipulation is never random. It follows patterns—often predictable ones—and it operates with specific tools that, once exposed, lose much of their power. In this chapter, we will break down the anatomy of manipulation, explain how it functions and provide guidance on recognizing it.

The Nature of Manipulation

Manipulation is about control. It twists communication and relationships away from mutual respect and toward domination and control. Where God invites, manipulation coerces. Where God offers freedom, manipulation binds. Where the Spirit brings clarity, manipulation clouds.

Techniques of Manipulation

Though the methods vary, several recurring techniques are easy to identify once we know them:

- Emotional Exploitation – pulling on guilt, fear, or pity to get compliance.

- Gaslighting – causing someone to doubt their own memory, perception, or sanity.

- Spiritualizing – wrapping harmful actions in religious language to shield them from critique.

- Withholding – using silence, exclusion, or the removal of affection to punish and pressure.

The Illusion of Benevolence

Manipulators often appear helpful or caring on the surface. They present themselves as protectors, mentors, or even spiritual guides, but beneath the surface, their aim is self-serving. Paul warned in 2 Corinthians 11:14-15 that even Satan "masquerades as an angel of light." Biblically, this is seen in the story of Judas Iscariot, who walked closely with Jesus and the disciples, appearing loyal and trustworthy, yet secretly plotted betrayal for personal gain.

In the world today, this is evident in public figures who build trust through moral or charitable appearances—such as a celebrity pastor exposed for using donations to fund a lavish lifestyle, or a corporate leader who promotes social responsibility while secretly exploiting workers or manipulating markets for personal gain. Their outward message seems noble, but their hidden motives reveal deception and self-interest.

The Uses of Power

Manipulation thrives where accountability is weak. It feeds on secrecy and flourishes in systems where leaders are unquestioned. In churches, workplaces, or families, manipulation grows when one person's word is treated as absolute.

Discernment at Work

Ephesians 5:11 instructs us to "have nothing to do with the fruitless deeds of darkness but rather expose them." By breaking down the anatomy of manipulation, we expose its weakness. Manipulation is powerful only when it goes unrecognized, but when exposed, it often collapses under its own weight.

Reflection Questions

- When have you seen manipulation disguised as care or guidance? How did you recognize it?

  _____

  _____

  _____

- Which of the listed techniques (emotional exploitation, gaslighting, spiritualizing, withholding) have you encountered most often?

  _____

  _____

  _____

- How does identifying manipulation patterns help reduce their power?

  _____

  _____

  _____

CHAPTER 2—*Reflection Questions*

- Where in your life or community might accountability need strengthening to resist manipulation?

  _____

  _____

  _____

- How does Ephesians 5:11 challenge you to respond when you recognize manipulation at work?

  _____

  _____

  _____

CHAPTER 3

THE WOLF IN SHEPHERD'S CLOTHING
Weaponizing Faith

Faith is meant to be life-giving, pointing us toward Christ, grounding us in truth, and building us up in love. Yet, history and Scripture alike warn us that faith can be twisted and weaponized for control, rather than nurtured for growth.

Biblical Examples of Weaponized Faith

The Bible doesn't shy away from exposing those who misuse religion for selfish gain. Eli's sons (1 Samuel 2:12-17) abused their priestly role, exploiting sacrifices meant for God to enrich themselves. The Pharisees (Matthew 23) burdened the people with heavy rules while neglecting justice, mercy, and faithfulness. Simon the sorcerer (Acts 8:9-23) sought to buy the power of the Holy Spirit for personal influence.

These accounts remind us that misusing faith is not a new phenomenon. Scripture provides both the warning and the clarity to recognize it.

Jesus warned of false prophets who come "in sheep's clothing, but inwardly, they are ferocious wolves" (Matthew 7:15). Weaponized faith looks righteous on the surface, but it devours those it touches.

Several years ago, a small congregation became captivated by a pastor who often preached with strong emotional appeals. At first, his passion drew people in. But over time, his sermons shifted. He began to use Scripture not to build up, but to pressure.

Members who questioned his decisions were reminded of the story of Korah's rebellion in Numbers 16, where those who opposed Moses were judged by God.

Slowly, disagreement was labeled as disobedience to God. Tithes and offerings were demanded with threats of being "cursed" if members withheld. Parents who hesitated to involve their children in every ministry program were told they were failing their spiritual duty. What began as zeal for God's Word became a web of fear, guilt, and control.

Many in the congregation remained silent, fearing public shaming. A few left quietly, carrying heavy spiritual wounds.

Looking back, what happened wasn't spiritual leadership, but spiritual weaponization. Scripture meant for guidance and encouragement was twisted into a tool of control.

The method of weaponizing faith often includes twisting Scripture to justify harmful practices, demanding loyalty to leaders rather than to Christ, using religious rituals as tools of manipulation, or instilling fear of spiritual consequences for disobedience.

Biblically, this pattern is evident throughout Scripture. The Pharisees in Jesus' time often distorted the Law to maintain their authority and influence. They elevated tradition over truth, placing impossible burdens on others while excusing their own hypocrisy (Matthew 23:23–24). Another example is King Saul, who used his God-given position to manipulate and pursue David out of jealousy and fear of losing power. Rather than leading through humility and obedience, Saul sought to preserve his throne through control and intimidation. Both examples reveal how spiritual authority can be corrupted when self-interest replaces submission to God.

In today's world, this same tactic appears in many forms. Some leaders exploit faith communities by twisting Scripture to demand unquestioning loyalty, discouraging members from thinking critically or seeking God for themselves. In extreme cases, cult-like groups use fear of divine punishment or eternal loss to control behavior and suppress dissent. Even within mainstream settings, some individuals use religion to advance personal agendas—whether through televangelists who prey on desperation for financial gain, or influencers who wrap self-promotion in spiritual language to appear anointed or chosen. Beyond the pulpit, faith is sometimes weaponized in politics, where select verses are quoted to justify discrimination, gain public favor, or stir division, even when those motives contradict the heart of the Gospel.

At its core, weaponized faith replaces the grace and freedom found in Christ with fear, guilt, and dependency on human authority. It creates an illusion of righteousness while corrupting the very message it claims to uphold. This is why Jesus repeatedly warned His followers to beware of false prophets who appear in sheep's clothing but inwardly are ravenous wolves—those who use the name of God not to heal, but to control.

When faith is weaponized, the results are devastating. Trust in God is undermined. Communities fracture under fear and suspicion, and believers are left anxious, spiritually wounded, and often driven from fellowship.

The Call to Discernment

The antidote to weaponized faith is discernment rooted in Scripture and guided by the Spirit. In 1 John 4:1, we are reminded, "Dear friends, do not believe every spirit, but test the spirits to see whether they are from God, because many false prophets have gone out into the world."

Discernment allows us to see past appearances, to test teachings and actions against the character of Christ. Healthy faith aligns with love, truth, and freedom. Weaponized faith produces fear, bondage, and confusion.

The Things the Lord Hates

Scripture not only shows us examples of corrupted faith but also makes clear what God detests. His hatred isn't random; it reflects His holiness and His love for what protects and preserves His people.

Proverbs 6:16-19 lists these plainly: "There are six things that the Lord hates, seven that are an abomination to him: haughty eyes, a lying tongue, hands that shed innocent blood, a heart that devises wicked plans, feet that make haste to run to evil, a false witness who breathes out lies, and one who sows discord among brothers."

Breaking It Down

- Haughty eyes (Pride) — Pride blinds us to our need for God and creates division. (James 4:6)

- A lying tongue — Lies align us with the enemy, the "father of lies." (John 8:44)
- Hands that Shed Innocent Blood — God sees every act of violence and injustice. (Genesis 4:10)
- A heart that devises wicked plans — Sin begins in the imagination before it becomes action. (Jeremiah 17:9)
- Feet quick to run to evil — Sin becomes destruction when pursued eagerly. (Isaiah 59:7)
- A false witness — Bearing false testimony destroys justice and reputations. (Exodus 20:16)
- One who sows discord — Division within God's people opposes His desire for unity. (Psalm 133:1)

Other Scriptures

- Malachi 2:16 — God hates unfaithfulness in covenant.
- Zechariah 8:17 — He hates evil plans and false oaths.
- Amos 5:21–23 — He despises empty worship without justice and righteousness.

Application: What God hates reveals what He loves: humility, truth, justice, unity, and sincerity of worship. Discernment is not only about spotting falsehoods in others, but also about aligning our own hearts with His.

Reflection Questions

- Which of these seven warnings do you most see at work in today's voices of culture, politics and religion? How can you respond in a way that aligns with God's heart?

- Which of the biblical examples of weaponized faith (Eli's sons, the Pharisees, Simon the sorcerer) speaks most strongly to you, and why?

- Have you ever witnessed faith being used as a tool for control? How did it impact those involved?

- What are some modern forms of weaponized faith you have seen in churches, communities, or media? How can you test spiritual messages or leaders against the character of Christ in practical ways?

  _____

  _____

  _____

- What steps can you take to ensure your own faith practices point people toward Christ rather than control?

  _____

  _____

  _____

CHAPTER 4

THE BIBLICAL FOUNDATION OF DISCERNMENT

*D*iscernment isn't simply suspicion or caution; it's a gift from God, rooted in His Word and made alive through His Spirit. True discernment helps us see clearly in a world clouded by deception and fear.

The Biblical Call to Discernment

Scripture repeatedly calls believers to discernment:

- Romans 12:2 – "Do not conform to the pattern of this world, but be transformed by the renewing of your mind. Then you will be able to test and approve what God's will is—His good, pleasing and perfect will."

- Hebrews 5:14 – "But solid food is for the mature, who by constant use have trained themselves to distinguish good from evil."

- 1 Thessalonians 5:21 – "But test them all; hold on to what is good."

Discernment is part of maturity. It grows as we train ourselves through God's Word, prayer, and obedience.

Peace in Discernment

Discernment should bring clarity and peace, not endless worry. While discernment sharpens our awareness, it's not meant to leave us anxious or suspicious. Philippians 4:7 reminds us, "And the peace of God, which transcends all understanding, will guard your hearts and your minds in Christ Jesus."

Sharing Discernment with Others

Sometimes, discernment reveals truths not just for us, but for others as well. When this happens, wisdom and gentleness are key. Discernment should never be wielded to shame or intimidate. Instead, it should serve as a tool to build up. Galatians 6:1 instructs us, "Brothers and sisters, if someone is caught in a sin, you who live by the Spirit should restore that person gently. But watch yourselves, or you also may be tempted."

Practical Ways to Grow in Discernment

- Regularly study Scripture for both knowledge and transformation.

  Don't just read for information—read to understand God's heart. The Word not only reveals truth but also trains your spirit to recognize deception when it appears disguised as good.

- Pray specifically for the Spirit's guidance when facing decisions or questionable teachings.

  The Holy Spirit is the believer's inner compass. Ask Him to reveal what aligns with God's will and what subtly leads away from it.

- Test teachings, practices, and influences against the character of Christ.

  If something produces pride, fear, confusion, or self-exaltation, it's likely not from God. True guidance always reflects humility, love, and truth consistent with Jesus' nature.

- Remain accountable to trusted believers who can offer a different perspective.

  God often confirms truth through community. Surround yourself with mature, honest believers who will lovingly challenge you when something doesn't align with Scripture.

Reflection Questions

- Which of the Scripture passages on discernment speaks to you most strongly, and why?

　

- Have you ever confused suspicion with discernment? What was the result?

　

- How can discernment and peace work together in your daily life?

CHAPTER 4—*Reflection Questions*

- When sharing discernment with others, what principles from Galatians 6:1 can guide you? What regular practices can you build into your life to strengthen discernment over time?

  _____

  _____

  _____

PART 2

EVERYDAY RESPONSES

CHAPTER 5

"IT'S JUST A DIFFERENCE OF OPINION"
Navigating Voices, Opinions, and Influencers

*I*n everyday life, disagreements and differing perspectives are unavoidable. Someone says, "It's just a difference of opinion," as though the phrase itself closes the discussion. But not all opinions are equal, and not all differences are harmless. Some carry the weight of truth, while others are shaped by manipulation, misinformation, or fear.

The Weight of Opinions

Opinions matter because they shape behavior. An opinion about health influences how someone treats their body. An opinion about politics affects how they vote. An opinion about faith impacts their eternal outlook. To dismiss opinions as "just" opinions underestimates their power.

Paul reminds us in 2 Corinthians 10:5 to "take captive every thought to make it obedient to Christ." Discernment requires us to test opinions—our own and others'—against the truth of God's Word. Some opinions may simply be preferences, but others touch on matters of justice, morality, or discipleship.

The Temptation of Relativism

In modern Western culture, relativism often cloaks itself in the language of tolerance. Relativism is the belief that truth and morality are not absolute but are shaped by individual perspective, culture, or circumstance. While phrases like "You have your truth, and I have mine" may sound peaceful or open-minded, they subtly erode the conviction that truth is objective, knowable, and rooted in God's Word. When truth becomes subjective, conviction weakens, and moral compromise becomes acceptable. To treat truth as optional is to diminish Christ Himself—for Jesus declared, "I am the way and the truth and the life" (John 14:6).

The Digital Arena: Opinions Online

In today's world, many of our "differences of opinion" don't just happen around the dinner table or at work. They play out on our feeds. Social media has become the new public square, and influencers shape the way millions think about politics, faith, relationships, and even what it means to live a "good life."

Here's the challenge: opinions online spread faster than the truth. Algorithms reward outrage, not accuracy. Posts that get the most clicks are often the ones that stir up fear or division. When someone says, "Relax, it's just an opinion," they often ignore the very real impact opinions have when they are broadcast to thousands or millions of followers.

Influencer culture especially blurs the line. A charismatic personality can make almost anything sound appealing, whether it's a product, an ideology, or a worldview. Many young people today admit they trust influencers more than traditional leaders. That kind of power, unchecked, can become manipulative.

Discernment in the digital arena means asking:

- Does this opinion align with Scripture, or just with culture?
- Is this influencer pointing me toward Christ or toward themselves?
- Am I being shaped by likes and shares, or by truth and wisdom?

Social media isn't evil—it can be a tool for encouragement, learning, and even spreading the gospel.

But it requires us to slow down, think critically, and remember that behind nearly every screen name is a soul.

What It Is Not

Discernment does not mean:

- Arguing endlessly with everyone who disagrees, and assuming every opposing view is demonic or malicious.

- Retreating into echo chambers where only familiar voices are heard, and confusing personal conviction with universal truth.

- Using faith as a weapon to win debates rather than to love others.

Discernment recognizes the difference between healthy dialogue and harmful distortion. It seeks clarity, not constant conflict. It pursues truth with humility, knowing only God sees perfectly.

Reflection Questions

- Have you ever dismissed something as "just an opinion" that turned out to have a real impact? What was the result?

  _____

  _____

  _____

- Where do you most often encounter the phrase "It's just a difference of opinion?" Is it in personal conversations, online, or elsewhere?

  _____

  _____

  _____

- How has social media or influencer culture shaped the way you and your peers form opinions? What practices can help you discern truth when scrolling through your feeds?

  _____

  _____

  _____

- How can you respond in love when opinions differ without compromising on truth?

_____

_____

_____

CHAPTER 6

THE FRUITS OF MANIPULATION

Manipulation doesn't remain hidden forever. Eventually, it produces fruit, and Jesus taught us "by their fruit you will recognize them. (Matthew 7:16) Examining the outcomes of manipulation helps us identify its presence and guard against its influence.

The Fruit of Confusion

Manipulation breeds confusion. Victims often feel uncertain, doubting themselves and their understanding. They replay conversations in their minds, second-guess decisions, and begin to distrust their own judgment. This fog of uncertainty makes them more dependent on the manipulator, who presents themselves as the only source of clarity.

In healthy relationships, open and effective communication fosters confidence. In manipulative systems, confusion is cultivated intentionally. The enemy is described in 1 Corinthians 14:33 as the author of disorder, but "God is not a God of disorder, but of peace."

The Fruit of Fear

Where Christ brings peace, manipulation thrives on fear. Fear becomes the silent chain that binds victims: fear of speaking up, fear of punishment, fear of being cast out, or fear of eternal consequences twisted by leaders.

This isn't the fear of the Lord that Scripture calls holy and life-giving. Instead, it's terror designed to control. As 1 John 4:18 declares, "There is no fear in love. But perfect love drives out fear." Manipulation replaces perfect love with perpetual fear, creating anxious, weary disciples.

The Fruit of Guilt and Shame

Manipulation often exploits guilt. Victims are told they are never doing enough, never faithful enough, never giving enough. Shame becomes a constant companion, distorting their identity as beloved children of God.

This is the opposite of the gospel, which says in Romans 8:1, "There is now no condemnation for those who are in Christ Jesus." Healthy conviction points us toward Christ's mercy; toxic shame keeps us chained to a false sense of unworthiness.

The Fruit of Division

Communities under manipulation fracture easily. Factions form, suspicion grows, and unity dissolves. People whisper in corners but avoid honest conversation. Friendships that once brought life become strained, as fear and mistrust erode what love once held together.

Jesus prayed in John 17:21 that His followers "may all be one." Manipulation works against this prayer, creating a divided and weakened body.

Victims of manipulation often carry emotional, spiritual, or even financial burdens they were never meant to bear. Leaders push them to give more, serve harder, or sacrifice endlessly — until exhaustion sets in, and the joy of serving God is replaced by a hollow weariness.

Jesus offers a different way: "Come to me, all you who are weary and burdened, and I will give you rest" (Matthew 11:28). Where manipulation drains life, Christ restores it.

When we step back, these fruits share a common pattern: they disorient, control and strip away identity. Victims lose sight of who God says they are and begin to live in the shadow of what manipulators demand. Instead of the Spirit's fruit, their lives bear the marks of oppression.

The Contrast: Fruit of the Spirit

Against these destructive fruits, Paul lists the fruit of the Spirit in Galatians 5:22–23: "love, joy, peace, forbearance, kindness, goodness, faithfulness, gentleness and self-control."

These are not abstract virtues, but lived realities:

- Love instead of fear
- Peace instead of confusion
- Joy instead of guilt and shame
- Unity instead of division
- Rest instead of burnout

The fruit of the Spirit reveals God's presence. The absence of these fruits — and the presence of confusion, fear, shame, division, and exhaustion — reveals manipulation.

Reflection Questions

- Which of the destructive fruits (confusion, fear, guilt/shame, division, burnout) have you seen most clearly in your community or past experiences?

  _____

  _____

  _____

- How do these destructive fruits connect back to the deeper patterns of fear, control, and loss of identity?

  _____

  _____

  _____

- What practical steps can you take to nurture the fruit of the Spirit in your own life?

  _____

  _____

  _____

- How does comparing destructive fruit to the fruit of the Spirit provide clarity in discernment?

- Where might God be calling you to step away from manipulation and toward freedom in Christ?

CHAPTER 7

THE COST OF SILENCE

*W*e've all been there: hearing something that doesn't sound right, seeing a situation that feels manipulative, or noticing someone being mistreated. And instead of speaking up, we stay silent. Silence may feel safer in the moment, but it comes with its own costs.

Silence in one moment makes silence in the next even easier. James 4:17 warns us: "If anyone, then, knows the good they ought to do and doesn't do it, it is sin for them."

When we remain silent in the face of distortion or harm, our discernment weakens. Every time we ignore the Spirit's nudge, it becomes harder to recognize His voice. Our conscience hardens. What once troubled us may start to feel "normal," and our courage shrinks.

Silence doesn't only affect us; it leaves others vulnerable. Victims of manipulation remain unsupported. They feel isolated, assuming no one will help, and withdraw in shame.

Abuse flourishes in silence. Harmful leaders go unchecked, and if no one speaks up, they grow bolder, believing their authority is unquestioned. Additionally, communities drift into confusion and fear. Anxiety spreads. People whisper privately, but never address issues openly.

Proverbs 31:8–9 calls us: "Speak up for those who cannot speak for themselves, for the rights of all who are destitute. Speak up and judge fairly; defend the rights of the poor and needy."

Perhaps most sobering, silence damages the credibility of our faith. When the church fails to speak against deception, abuse, or injustice, the world concludes that Christ approves. Ezekiel 33:7-8 describes God's charge to the watchman: "if he fails to warn of danger, the blood of the people is on his hands." In the same way, when believers stay quiet in the face of corruption, God's name is dishonored.

When Speaking Up Feels Impossible

Speaking up isn't always simple. It requires wisdom and timing. Practical ways to begin:

- Pray first for courage and clarity.
- Start small with a gentle question: "What do you mean by that?"
- Seek allies. Don't speak up alone if possible.

- Be anchored in Scripture as your foundation.

The Alternative: Courageous Love

Silence carries a cost, but speaking up brings freedom. Jesus confronted leaders who distorted truth (Matthew 23). Paul confronted Peter when his actions compromised the gospel (Galatians 2:11-14). Speaking up isn't about winning arguments, but about love for truth, for the vulnerable, and for Christ.

Reflection Questions

- Can you recall a time when you stayed silent in the face of something wrong? What did it cost you?

    _____

    _____

    _____

- Have you ever seen silence allow manipulation or abuse to continue unchecked? How did it affect the community?

    _____

    _____

    _____

- Which of the costs (to self, to others, to Christ's witness) challenges you most deeply?

    _____

    _____

    _____

- What small step could you take to begin speaking up with wisdom and love?

- How does Jesus's example challenge the idea that silence is always safer?

PART
3

THE CULTURAL CHALLENGE OF NATIONALISM

CHAPTER 8

THE UNSETTLING FUSION

The blending of faith and politics isn't new, but it has taken on new intensity in recent years. For many, Christianity has become intertwined with cultural and national identity, where being a "good Christian" is often equated with being a "good citizen" or aligning with a particular political party. This fusion can be subtle at first—rooted in a genuine desire to uphold moral values or preserve national stability—but over time it can distort both the message of the Gospel and the mission of the Church. When faith becomes a political badge rather than a living relationship with Christ, the cross is replaced with ideology.

This unsettling mixture often leads to a selective form of Christianity that prioritizes power, nationalism, or cultural dominance over humility, justice, and compassion. Instead of shaping the world through Christlike love and truth, believers risk allowing worldly systems and partisan agendas to shape their faith. History and Scripture both show that whenever the Church seeks influence through political might rather than spiritual integrity, it loses its prophetic voice. The result is a faith diluted by allegiance to human kingdoms rather than the Kingdom of God.

The Temptation of Power

From the beginning, God's people have been tempted to grasp political power as a shortcut to security and influence. Israel wanted a king "like the other nations" (1 Samuel 8:5), despite God's warning that such power would lead to oppression. Later, many in Israel longed for a Messiah who would overthrow Rome and restore national dominance, missing that Jesus came to establish a spiritual kingdom, not a political one. Even the early Church faced pressure to compromise with governing powers for the sake of safety and acceptance. Yet, the apostles chose obedience to God over allegiance to earthly rulers (Acts 5:29).

The temptation to trust human authority over God's reign remains with us today. In modern times, this is evident when believers place their hope in political figures to "save" the nation, equating moral revival with electoral victory. Churches sometimes mirror partisan agendas more than the teachings of Christ, allowing nationalism, ideology, or cultural battles to define their mission. While political involvement has its place, Scripture reminds us that no system, party, or leader can substitute for the righteousness, justice, and peace that come from God alone.

The False Promise of Nationalism

When faith and nationalism fuse, the church's mission is distorted. Instead of being salt and light, it becomes a tool of political agendas. Nationalism tells us that salvation lies in the strength of a nation, the dominance of a culture, or the victory of a political movement. But Scripture insists that our hope is in Christ alone. Psalm 146:3 reminds us, "Do not put your trust in princes, in human beings, who cannot save."

We see this unsettling fusion when faith is equated with loyalty to a political party or nation, or when Scripture is selectively used to endorse policies or leaders. We also see it when Christian identity is tied more to cultural symbols than to Christ, or the church defends power rather than the vulnerable.

The fusion of faith and nationalism isn't a harmless partnership. It reshapes the gospel into something unrecognizable. Instead of Christ at the center, the nation or culture takes His place.

The purpose of this section isn't to demonize political involvement. Christians are called to engage in civic life. Still, that engagement must be rooted in Christ's Kingdom, not in the idol of nationalism.

A Note on Nationalism and Discernment

In this book, White Christian Nationalism (WCN) and Right-wing Christian Nationalism (RCN) are used as primary examples of how faith can be distorted and weaponized for political and cultural power. These movements are current, recognizable, and deeply relevant to the times in which we live.

The misuse of faith through nationalism isn't limited to these expressions alone. History has shown, and the future will likely show again, that whenever religious devotion is merged with political or cultural identity in a way that distorts the gospel, the same dangers arise: pride, division, manipulation, and injustice.

Whether it takes the form of WCN, RCN, or another yet-to-emerge movement, the call to discernment remains the same. Our allegiance must always be to Christ above all, not to any earthly ideology that claims His name but denies His truth.

Reflection Questions

- Where have you seen Christianity equated with nationalism in your context?

  _____

  _____

  _____

- How does the story of Israel's demand for a king in 1 Samuel 8 parallel today's temptations?

  _____

  _____

  _____

- What are some dangers of putting ultimate hope in political systems or leaders?

  _____

  _____

  _____

- How can you discern whether your faith engagement is rooted in Christ or fused with nationalism?

- What practices can keep Christ, rather than culture or politics, at the center of your faith?

CHAPTER 9

Defining the Doctrine
WHAT IS WHITE CHRISTIAN NATIONALISM?

In recent years, the phrase White Christian Nationalism (WCN) has moved from scholarly journals into public conversation. It is often invoked as both an accusation and an alarm, yet many believers remain uncertain about its true meaning. Clarifying this doctrine is essential because misused labels can harm unity, but unexamined ideologies can corrupt one's witness. To discern rightly, the Church must define WCN not as a partisan slogan but as a worldview—one that entwines racial identity, national destiny, and divine favor into a single, often distorted narrative (Perry & Whitehead, 2020). Scripture reminds us that "my kingdom is not of this world" (John 18:36), and any teaching that blurs that boundary requires careful examination.

Historical Roots

The seeds of WCN reach deep into early American soil. Seventeenth-century Puritans carried a covenantal imagination, believing the colonies were a new Israel tasked with building a city upon a hill. While this aspiration fostered compassion and community, it also linked divine blessing to social order and, eventually, to whiteness as a moral norm (Noll, 2002).

By the nineteenth century, this theology had merged with Manifest Destiny—the conviction that God had ordained the expansion of Anglo-Protestant civilization across the continent (Horsman, 1981). Religious rhetoric justified conquest, slavery, and the removal of Indigenous peoples under the banner of providence. Sermons portrayed national success as proof of divine election, and failure as judgment for disobedience.

After the Civil War, a wounded national conscience sought healing through a sacralized patriotism. White churches in both North and South often framed racial hierarchy as part of God's design, baptizing social dominance as moral order (Emerson & Smith, 2000). The twentieth century carried these assumptions forward through the Cold War's civil-religious revival: "under God" entered the Pledge, "In God We Trust" appeared on currency, and Christianity fused with civic virtue. Though many believers meant this sincerely, it subtly taught generations that to be a good American was to be a Christian, and to be a good Christian was to be white and patriotic.

Core Beliefs and Characteristics

White Christian Nationalism is not a denomination but a fusion ideology. It blends ethnocentric loyalty, cultural nostalgia, and selective theology into a moral vision of nationhood. Its distinguishing claims include:

- Divine Election of the Nation – The belief that the United States has a special covenant with God, comparable to ancient Israel. This idea confuses divine providence with political exceptionalism, implying that God's promises depend on national obedience rather than Christ's finished work.

- Sanctified Identity – Whiteness becomes an unspoken standard of righteousness. Cultural traits of European Christianity—such as dress, language, and worship style—are often treated as inherently biblical. Scripture, however, celebrates the multi-ethnic body of Christ where "there is neither Jew nor Gentile… for you are all one in Christ Jesus" (Galatians 3:28).

- Moral Restorationism – A longing for a mythical past when the nation was "Christian." This nostalgia ignores the moral failures of that era and idealizes social hierarchies that excluded many believers of color (Butler, 2021).

- Power as Proof of Faith – The assumption that political dominance signals divine blessing. Yet the cross teaches that weakness and service, not control, mark the kingdom's advance (Phil. 2:5-8).

- Apocalyptic Fear of Loss – Anxiety that demographic or cultural change equals persecution. This fear often fuels anger rather than repentance and a mission.

Sociologists observe that WCN functions less as theology and more as a cultural identity marker (Perry & Whitehead, 2020). It grants belonging and moral certainty in uncertain times, offering an identity that feels holy precisely because it confuses culture with covenant.

Modern Expressions and Research Findings

Contemporary studies reveal how these ideas shape attitudes toward race, immigration, and politics. Perry and Whitehead (2020) found that high adherence to WCN is correlated with stronger opposition to racial equality measures, more restrictive views on immigration, and greater tolerance for authoritarian leaders. Their research suggests that WCN operates as a "deep story," interpreting national decline as a spiritual rebellion.

Gorski (2017) describes this as American Civil Religion Revised—a fusion of biblical language and nationalist myth that replaces covenant with contract: God blesses America if America defends a particular cultural order. This logic undergirds slogans like "take our country back" or "restore

Christian America." It frames faith as a defensive fortress rather than a missionary calling.

Historically, similar fusions emerged in other nations where the majority religion aligned with ethnicity and power. The German "Deutsche Christen" movement of the 1930s and South Africa's apartheid theology illustrate how baptized nationalism can deform both church and conscience (De Gruchy, 1986). WCN participates in this lineage, though in a uniquely American form.

Perry and Gorski (2022) further note that WCN's resilience stems from its adaptability: it can speak the language of revival one decade and that of populism the next. It borrows biblical metaphors of warfare and purity but directs them toward human enemies instead of spiritual ones (Ephesians 6:12).

Media ecosystems reinforce this fusion. Cable networks and social platforms create what researchers call epistemic enclaves—closed loops where fear narratives and patriotic hymns coexist as worship (Brooks, 2019). The result is a religious nationalism that feels simultaneously righteous and embattled.

Biblical and Theological Evaluation

Scripture consistently distinguishes between allegiance to God and allegiance to empire. When Israel demanded a king "like the nations," the Lord warned that political power would enslave their sons and daughters (1 Samuel 8:10-18). Jesus echoed this warning, declaring, "Render to Caesar the things that are Caesar's, and to God the things that are God's" (Mark 12:17). The early church thrived under governments hostile to its faith precisely because its hope was not national but eternal (Hebrews 11:13-16).

WCN distorts several key doctrines:

- The Kingdom of God – God's reign is universal and spiritual, not geographic. It transcends borders and ethnicities (Luke 13:29).

- Election – In Christ, election is corporate and gracious, not ethnic or political (Ephesians 1:4-6).

- Mission – The Great Commission sends disciples to all nations, not to exalt one nation above others (Matthew 28:19-20).

- Unity of the Body – Paul rebuked early believers who divided along cultural lines (1 Corinthians 1:12-13). Any teaching that privileges one culture violates the gospel's reconciling purpose.

Theologically, nationalism becomes idolatry when love of the nation surpasses love of neighbor. Augustine called this *ordo amoris*—disordered love—where good affections become destructive when misplaced (Augustine, City of

God, XIX). The psalmist's cry, "Blessed is the nation whose God is the Lord" (Psalm 33:12), was never a charter for supremacy but a call to righteousness defined by justice and mercy (Micah 6:8).

Pastoral Reflection and Call to Discernment

The Church must respond neither with denial nor despair but with discernment rooted in love. Denial ignores the ways WCN has shaped congregations; despair forgets that Christ still reforms His people. True repentance requires naming the idol before it can be cast down.

Pastors can begin by teaching historical literacy—helping believers trace how faith has been used and misused in national narratives. Congregations should celebrate multi-ethnic fellowship as a foretaste of heaven (Revelation 7:9) and emphasize the global Church that thrives far beyond American borders.

Discipleship must also address the emotional drivers of nationalism: fear, nostalgia, and resentment. The antidote to fear is perfect love (1 John 4:18); the cure for nostalgia is gratitude for what God is doing now; the remedy for resentment is the humility of Christ, "who made himself nothing, taking the nature of a servant" (Philippians 2:7).

As believers learn to test every spirit (1 John 4:1) and every narrative by the fruit of the Spirit (Galatians 5:22-23), they rediscover that discernment is not suspicion—it is peace. The Shepherd's voice is never the loudest in the public square, but it is always the one that leads toward love.

Scriptural Response

The Bible speaks clearly against these distortions:

- Galatians 3:28 – "There is neither Jew nor Gentile, neither slave nor free, nor is there male and female, for you are all one in Christ Jesus."

- Philippians 3:20 – "But our citizenship is in heaven. And we eagerly await a Savior from there, the Lord Jesus Christ."

- Acts 10:34–35 – "God does not show favoritism but accepts from every nation the one who fears him and does what is right."

Reflection Questions

- Why is it important to distinguish between patriotism and White Christian Nationalism?

\

\

\

- How have you seen WCN distort the witness of the church in your context?

\

\

\

- What historical examples of WCN's influence stand out to you? How do the Scriptures above correct the false theology of WCN?

\

\

\

- What practices can help keep Christ, rather than race or nation, at the center of faith?

　_____

　_____

　_____

CHAPTER 10

Defining the Doctrine
WHAT IS RIGHT-WING CHRISTIAN NATIONALISM?

*I*n the previous chapter, we examined White Christian Nationalism as a fusion of racial identity and divine destiny. Yet not all Christian nationalism is overtly racial. Right-Wing Christian Nationalism (RCN) often arises from the same soil. Still, it grows in a slightly different direction—rooted less in whiteness and more in ideology. It wraps theological language around political loyalty, trading racial purity for cultural uniformity and replacing grace with grievance.

Right-Wing Christian Nationalism claims to defend "biblical values," but it often narrows those values to a handful of political issues while neglecting the holistic ethic of Jesus: love of God and neighbor (Matthew 22:37–39). Like WCN, it blurs the line between the Kingdom of God and the kingdoms of men, assuming the health of the Church depends on the power of the state.

As theologian Miroslav Volf (1996) observed, when faith aligns itself too closely with coercive power, "the cross is eclipsed by the sword." This chapter traces the historical development of RCN, examines the beliefs that sustain it, and explains how Christians can discern the difference between cultural conservatism and Christ-centered conviction.

Historical Context and Political Development

Right-Wing Christian Nationalism in the United States has its modern roots in the mid-twentieth century, when conservative evangelicals began to see political engagement as a spiritual duty. In the 1950s, leaders like Billy Graham and Dwight Eisenhower's administration promoted a vague "Judeo-Christian" identity as an antidote to atheistic communism (Herzog, 2010). Religion became a civic rallying point, and patriotism became a proxy for piety.

The real ideological fusion, however, took shape during the late 1970s and 1980s with the rise of the Moral Majority and the Religious Right. Jerry Falwell Sr., Pat Robertson, and other leaders mobilized millions of conservative Christians to influence legislation on abortion, education, and family values (Martin, 1996). This movement, while initially motivated by moral concern, gradually merged theological authority with partisan loyalty. Political victory began to feel synonymous with divine favor.

RCN differs from traditional conservatism. Classic political conservatism values limited government and moral order, but

RCN adds a religious absolutism that treats political opponents as enemies of God. Historian Kristin Kobes Du Mez (2020) notes that this ideology was often reinforced by a "militant masculinity" that defined spiritual strength in terms of aggression and control rather than humility and service.

After the September 11, 2001, attacks, nationalism in America took on renewed religious fervor. Evangelical symbols and language were frequently used in speeches about foreign policy and war, framing national defense as a moral crusade (Marsden, 2006). As global terrorism was cast in apocalyptic tones, the rhetoric of righteousness again became entangled with the machinery of the state. The 2016 election cycle then amplified this trend, with social media creating echo chambers where political identity became synonymous with Christian identity (Jones, 2016).

By the 2020s, Right-Wing Christian Nationalism had evolved into a digital movement, uniting populist politics, online prophecy ministries, and apocalyptic fear narratives (Stewart, 2021). It declared itself the "last bastion of biblical truth" in a fallen world but often measured faith by the volume of outrage rather than the depth of obedience.

Core Beliefs and Distortions

Right-Wing Christian Nationalism carries several recurring themes that distort the gospel's message. While many adherents sincerely love Christ and their country, these core beliefs redirect devotion from the Savior to a system.

The Myth of the Chosen Party RCN sanctifies partisan loyalty. Political platforms are treated as sacred texts, and leaders are portrayed as anointed messengers of God's will. This replaces biblical discernment with ideological conformity. As Isaiah warned, "Woe to those who call evil good and good evil" (Isaiah 5:20). True righteousness cannot be legislated by allegiance to any earthly party.

Moral Reductionism

The gospel is reduced to a handful of social issues, often revolving around sexuality, family, and nationalism. Complex biblical imperatives—justice, mercy, humility, care for the poor—are sidelined as "liberal distractions" (Galli, 2019). Yet Jesus consistently defined faithfulness through compassion and truth, not selective outrage (Matthew 23:23).

Apocalyptic Politics

RCN often frames political struggles as cosmic warfare between good and evil. Opponents are not merely misguided but demonized. This fosters spiritual anxiety and hostility rather than faith and love (1 John 4:18). The symbolism of the beast and empire in the Book of Revelation becomes weaponized to label modern adversaries rather than to critique power itself (Bauckham, 1993).

The Prosperity of Power

Like the prosperity gospel, RCN equates success with divine approval. Victories at the ballot box are viewed as signs of God's favor; losses as proof of corruption or persecution. However, Scripture reveals that God's people thrive most under humility and suffering, not dominance (2 Corinthians 12:9).

Cultural Idolatry

Many RCN adherents conflate Western culture with Christianity. The result is cultural imperialism masquerading as a form of evangelism. Christ, however, transcends culture. The Church's beauty lies in diversity, not uniformity (Revelation 7:9).

RCN's theology of power thus mirrors the world's logic more than the gospel's wisdom. It offers believers a sense of belonging and purpose, but at the cost of the kingdom's distinctiveness.

Modern Expressions and Research Findings

Sociological studies confirm that RCN is a potent force shaping U.S. religion and politics. Whitehead and Perry

(2020) identify a cluster of beliefs that define Christian nationalism: the conviction that the federal government should declare the U.S. a Christian nation, that prayer should be mandated in schools, and that America's success reflects divine blessing. These attitudes correlate strongly with authoritarian views and resistance to pluralism.

Political scientist Andrew Whitehead (2021) distinguishes between "cultural evangelicals," whose faith identity is primarily political, and "devotional evangelicals," whose lives are rooted in personal discipleship. RCN often captures the former, transforming belief into brand. Studies by the Pew Research Center (2018) show that such identification predicts higher support for militaristic policies, skepticism toward immigration, and alignment with conspiracy narratives.

Digital media has accelerated these dynamics. Platforms like YouTube and Telegram host networks of self-styled "prophets" who blend political commentary with eschatology. They frame elections as spiritual showdowns and dissenters as apostates (Stewart, 2021). This ecosystem creates a feedback loop where political rhetoric is baptized in apocalyptic urgency.

Historian John Fea (2018) calls this phenomenon "the age of fear," noting that it thrives on the belief that Christianity's survival depends on cultural control. Fear replaces faith as the organizing principle. Yet Jesus warned

His disciples not to be afraid even when the world opposed them (John 16:33).

The global picture highlights the uniqueness and peril of RCN's influence. In contrast, Christians in many nations flourish as creative minorities, embodying faith without political dominance. The American Church must rediscover that same posture of witness rather than warfare.

Biblical and Theological Evaluation

The central error of Right-Wing Christian Nationalism is not love of country but confusion of kingdoms. Scripture affirms the goodness of civic duty (Rom. 13:1–7) but never equates national triumph with divine truth. The early church's loyalty to Christ placed it in tension with the empire, rather than in partnership with it (Acts 5:29).

Distortion of Power

Jesus redefined power through the cross. He refused Satan's offer of "all the kingdoms of the world" (Matthew 4:8–10). His kingdom is established not by coercion but by cruciform love. When Christians use political force to advance spiritual aims, they risk betraying the very model of leadership they espouse.

Misuse of Prophecy

RCN often appropriates prophetic language to endorse leaders or policies. Yet biblical prophecy speaks truth to power, not on behalf of it. Nathan confronted David's sin; he did not justify it (2 Samuel 12:1–7). Amos rebuked nations for injustice, reminding them that religious zeal without righteousness is offensive to God (Amos 5:21–24).

Ethical Fragmentation

Paul's exhortation to Timothy remains relevant: "The Lord's servant must not be quarrelsome but kind to everyone, able to teach, not resentful" (2 Tim. 2:24). When believers adopt the rhetoric of culture wars, they forfeit gentleness, the very fruit that authenticates the Spirit's work (Galatians 5:22–23).

The Church's prophetic witness depends on its independence. When it becomes a chaplain to one ideology, it loses the capacity to correct that ideology's sin. Jesus warned that salt without distinctiveness is "no longer good for anything" (Matthew 5:13).

Pastoral Reflection and Call to Discernment

Pastors today face the delicate challenge of shepherding congregations divided by politics yet united by baptism. The goal is not political neutrality but gospel fidelity. Neutrality avoids conflict; fidelity speaks truth in love. Leaders must teach believers to engage civically without confusing civic engagement with discipleship.

Practical steps include:

- Teaching political humility. Remind believers that no party embodies the Kingdom's fullness.

- Re-centering on Scripture. Encourage study that prioritizes Christ's commands over partisan commentary.

- Cultivating empathy. Create spaces where Christians can listen to believers with different perspectives, modeling the patience of Christ.

- Restoring worship. When God's presence becomes more captivating than political spectacle, hearts recalibrate toward peace.

Ultimately, the Church's power lies not in ballots but in the Beatitudes. Blessed are the peacemakers, the meek, the merciful (Matthew 5:3–10). The Shepherd still calls His flock to follow a narrow road marked by humility, not dominance.

As RCN fades—as all earthly movements do—the gospel endures. The task of the believer is not to preserve cultural supremacy but to bear faithful witness until Christ's kingdom fully comes.

Reflection Questions

- How does RCN differ from simply holding conservative political convictions?

  _____

  _____

  _____

- In what ways have you observed RCN's impact on Christian unity and witness?

  _____

  _____

  _____

- Which of the Scriptures above most clearly challenges the assumptions of RCN?

  _____

  _____

  _____

CHAPTER 10—*Reflection Questions*

- What dangers arise when political loyalty becomes a test of Christian faith?

- How can Christians engage politically without confusing the gospel with ideology?

CHAPTER 11

THE SEDUCTION OF NATIONALISM
Why It Appeals to Believers

Nationalism, whether framed in racial or political terms, doesn't only gain its power through leaders or systems. It gains power because it appeals to the longings of ordinary believers. Understanding these longings helps us see why so many are drawn in and why the gospel provides a better answer.

After exploring the visible forms of Christian nationalism, we must pause to listen beneath the noise—to the inner ache that makes such movements feel holy. Political theologies seldom begin as conspiracies; they begin as longings. Every idol begins as a hunger for something real. The appeal of nationalism among believers cannot be understood only by history or ideology; it must be understood by the heart.

Augustine wrote that the human heart "is restless until it rests in Thee" (Confessions, I.1). When that restlessness attaches itself to the homeland instead of heaven, patriotism quietly becomes piety. The banners that once marked civic pride begin to resemble banners of praise. And because the longing for belonging is among humanity's deepest desires, the seduction feels righteous.

The Longing for Belonging

Every soul yearns for home. Scripture itself is the story of exile and return—from Eden to Egypt, from Babylon to the New Jerusalem. The people of God have always sung songs of the homeland (Psalm 137:1-6). Nationalism whispers to that ache, promising a visible kingdom we can protect with our hands.

For many believers, especially in cultures where faith feels marginalized, nationalism offers community when church fellowship feels thin. It promises meaning through mission—"defend the nation," "save our culture." Sociologists refer to this as a substitute ecclesia, a political fellowship that performs the emotional work of a church (Whitehead & Perry, 2020).

The appeal deepens because nationalism wraps belonging in memory. It sanctifies nostalgia—the conviction that once, long ago, faith and nation walked hand in hand. The imagination of a "Christian America" functions like a lost Eden. Its recovery becomes an act of redemption.

But nostalgia is a poor historian. The era it romanticizes often excluded the very neighbors Jesus commanded us to love. The gospel calls believers not backward to an idealized past but forward to a redeemed future (Revelation 21:1-5).

The Fear of Loss

If belonging is the promise, fear is the price. Fear of cultural decline, of moral confusion, of children growing up in a world we no longer recognize. Fear is powerful because it disguises itself as vigilance. Yet Scripture warns that fear, not faith, is the root of idolatry (1 John 4:18).

Right-Wing Christian Nationalism thrives in anxious times because it offers control where faith demands trust. It baptizes the instinct to defend, assuring believers that vigilance equals virtue. But the kingdom Jesus described is never threatened by the winds of politics; it is "not of this world" (John 18:36).

Sociologist Robert Bellah (1967) noted that civil religion often emerges when nations seek reassurance of divine favor during upheaval. The flag becomes the sacrament of security for weary hearts that feel safer than the unseen sovereignty of God.

The Language of Heaven, the Tools of Earth

Nationalism borrows the words of worship. It speaks of "revival," "calling," "faithful remnant," yet wields the tools of coercion and outrage. It is seductive precisely because it sounds scriptural.

The serpent in Genesis did not offer rebellion; he offered clarity—"You will be like God, knowing good and evil" (Genesis 3:5). Nationalism offers the same temptation: certainty without surrender. It tells believers they can preserve righteousness through legislation alone.

The prophets of Israel warned against this confusion. When Judah trusted military alliances rather than mercy, Isaiah declared, "In returning and rest you shall be saved; in quietness and trust shall be your strength" (Isaiah 30:15). Yet the people preferred horses and chariots. So do we.

Faith that seeks to win rather than serve ceases to be faith. Jesus refused both the zealot's sword and the Pharisee's purity tests; He chose the towel and the table (John 13:3-15). The tools of the earth can defend borders, but they cannot build a kingdom.

The Theological Roots of the Seduction

At its core, nationalism distorts two sound doctrines: incarnation and mission.

- Incarnation Misunderstood – God's choice to dwell among us affirms the material world. Yet nationalism inverts this truth, claiming that one culture or nation uniquely embodies divine favor. The Word became flesh in a particular body, not to sanctify that body's ethnicity but to redeem all flesh (John 1:14; Philippians 2:6-8).

- Mission Misapplied – The Great Commission sends disciples to the nations, not to exalt one nation above others (Matthew 28:19-20). When the mission becomes maintenance of culture, evangelism withers into propaganda.

Theologian N. T. Wright (2012) warns that the Church must never mistake the symbols of Caesar for the reign of Christ. To do so is to "trade resurrection hope for empire nostalgia." The seduction is subtle because it plays upon virtues—gratitude, stewardship, and loyalty—but turns them inward, until love of neighbor becomes suspicion of the stranger.

Contemporary Manifestations

Today, the seduction is amplified by the hum of algorithms. Social media rewards outrage, and outrage feels like conviction. Videos promise revelation: hidden enemies, moral emergencies, urgent calls to prayer that sound more like calls to arms. Many believers enter these spaces seeking truth, but they stay for the adrenaline rush of certainty.

Psychologists describe this as dopamine discipleship—the emotional high of being "in the know" (McCracken, 2021). Yet Jesus said His followers would be known by love, not by being right (John 13:35). The Spirit's fruit is peace, patience, and gentleness—qualities that seldom trend.

Churches, too, can echo the seduction when sermons trade gospel for grievance. Congregations become coalitions, pulpits become podiums. In such moments, the Bride of Christ risks becoming the mouthpiece of fear rather than the herald of hope.

The Invitation of Jesus

Against every counterfeit kingdom, Jesus still offers the same invitation He gave to anxious disciples on a stormy sea: "It is I; do not be afraid" (John 6:20). The calm He brings is not the stillness of control but the peace of surrender.

He invites His people to rediscover a holy detachment—a love for their nation that is grateful yet not possessive, critical yet not cynical. Jeremiah told the exiles to "seek the peace of the city… and pray to the Lord for it" (Jeremiah 29:7). That posture remains the model: faithfulness in exile, not domination in triumph.

When believers anchor identity in the Kingdom that cannot be shaken (Hebrews 12:28), the seduction of nationalism loses its voice. The anthem of heaven is louder.

Pastoral Reflection and Restoration

Healing from this seduction requires patience and gentleness. Hearts drawn to nationalism are rarely hardened; they are frightened, longing for stability in a shifting world. Shepherds must lead not with shame but with understanding.

Practical steps include:

- Confession and Teaching. Invite honest reflection on where political passion has overshadowed compassion.

- Story and Testimony. Share accounts of believers worldwide who live faithfully without national privilege—proof that the gospel does not depend on power.

- Re-enchant Worship. Center gatherings on awe, not anxiety. When worship recovers wonder, fear loses oxygen.

- Renew Community. Encourage small acts of local mercy—such as feeding, visiting, and welcoming. These are the politics of the Kingdom.

As the Church learns again to love without labeling, the Spirit will purify her witness. The Shepherd's voice is tender, but it is not naive. He calls His flock away from idols that promise safety and toward the risky peace of love.

The anthem of nationalism says, We will not be replaced.

The song of the Lamb replies, You are already redeemed.

Reflection Questions

- Which of these resonates most with you? Why? Have you seen nationalism appeal to these longings in your community or church?

  _____

  _____

  _____

- How does the gospel provide a more lasting answer to each longing?

  _____

  _____

  _____

- What Scriptures can you hold onto when tempted to seek belonging or security in nationalism?

  _____

  _____

  _____

- How can we lovingly redirect others when they pursue these longings in nationalism rather than Christ?

_____

_____

_____

CHAPTER 12

RESTORING THE WITNESS
A Church Set Apart for the Kingdom

If nationalism's seduction distorts our vision, then restoration begins with sight—seeing again what the Church was meant to be. After fear has shouted its slogans and pride has worn itself thin, a quieter question remains: Who are we, really, when no flag waves above us?

Jesus answered with simplicity that still startles the world: "You are the light of the world. A city set on a hill cannot be hidden" (Matthew 5:14). The Church's vocation is illumination, not domination. The light that draws others does not burn; it warms. Restoring the witness of Christ's body means returning to that kind of light.

Remembering the Original Calling

From Abraham onward, God's people were chosen not for privilege but for purpose—"that all the families of the earth shall be blessed" (Genesis 12:3). Election was never an exemption from humility but a commission to service.

Israel's law instructed care for the stranger because "you were strangers in Egypt" (Deuteronomy 10:19). The early Church carried that same ethic into the Roman Empire, feeding plague victims, rescuing exposed infants, and welcoming foreigners. Their allegiance was unmistakably heavenly, yet their love was unmistakably earthly.

Restoration begins when modern believers remember that heritage. We are not guardians of a fortress but stewards of a table.

Recovering a Theology of Weakness

The kingdoms of the world celebrate strength; the Kingdom of God delights in weakness redeemed. Paul boasted only in his infirmities, "that the power of Christ may rest upon me" (2 Cor. 12:9). When the Church forgets this paradox, she grasps for the world's tools—platforms, influence, coercion—and loses her prophetic power.

Theologian Jürgen Moltmann (1972) wrote that hope is born "from the cross, not the sword." The witness of a crucified Messiah unmasks every empire that seeks salvation through dominance. To restore the witness is therefore to embrace again the scandal of humility: to choose service over supremacy, empathy over efficiency, presence over performance.

Relearning Hospitality in a Hostile Age

Nationalism closes borders of the heart; the gospel opens doors. In Acts 2, the Spirit fell upon believers of every tongue, erasing boundaries through the power of comprehension. The first miracle of the Church was not conquest but communication. To be filled with the Spirit is to speak peace in another's language.

In a divided culture, hospitality becomes a revolution of gentleness. It means listening longer than we argue, feeding before we correct, and remembering that every guest carries the image of God. Hebrews 13:2 reminds us that some have "entertained angels unawares." Restored witness begins around such tables.

Practical expressions may look small: a congregation partnering with a mosque for community service; believers defending the dignity of immigrants; Christians confessing historic wrongs and making restitution. These are sacraments of credibility. They tell the watching world that Jesus has a different kind of power.

Renewing Worship and Word

When the Church's songs sound more like anthems of fear than psalms of trust, worship must be healed. True worship recenters our gaze on God's holiness rather than the nation's headlines. It trains the imagination to see the

Lamb on the throne instead of any candidate on a platform (Revelation 5:6).

Likewise, the Word must be read as revelation, not ammunition. Pastors and teachers can model exegesis that asks, What is God saying to us? Before asking, how can this verse defend us? Scripture forms citizens of heaven who bless their earthly cities without idolizing them.

When worship and Word converge in humility, discipleship produces discernment. The Church becomes less reactive and more radiant.

Rebuilding Trust Through Truth and Transparency

Restoration also requires repentance at institutional levels. Churches that have become entangled with the political machinery must openly acknowledge that entanglement. Confession is not weakness; it is the beginning of credibility (1 John 1:9).

Transparency about finances, alliances, and public witness restores confidence that the Church's mission is Christ's kingdom alone. Sociologist Robert Putnam (2020) found that communal trust grows where institutions practice visible accountability. For the Church, that accountability is spiritual: every elder and pastor is a steward, not an owner, of influence.

Reimagining Mission for a Global Church

The twenty-first-century Church is the most global body in history. Christianity's demographic center has shifted south and east—to Africa, Latin America, and Asia (Jenkins, 2011). This global reality undermines every nationalist fantasy. The Spirit is already building a family too vast for any flag.

To restore witness in the West is therefore to learn again from the rest. From African communities that pray through persecution, from Asian house churches that multiply under pressure, from Latin congregations whose joy thrives amid scarcity. These testimonies remind us that power is not a prerequisite for faithfulness.

Mission must be mutual, not managerial. The Church in America regains her soul when she kneels to receive rather than rises to command.

The Biblical Vision of a Set-Apart People

Peter called believers "a chosen race, a royal priesthood, a holy nation" (1 Peter 2:9)—language that can easily be misused by nationalists. Yet the next verse defines that nation's vocation: "that you may declare the praises of Him who called you out of darkness." The Church is a nation of light, dispersed among earthly nations for witness, not conquest.

John's Revelation closes history not with one empire enthroned but with every tribe and tongue gathered before the Lamb (Revelation 7:9). That is the nation to which we ultimately belong. Restoring the witness means living now as citizens of that future city whose builder is God (Hebrews 11:10).

Reflection and Commission

Every generation of believers must relearn how to be in the world but not of it (John 17:14-18). The task is perennial: to love the homeland without worshiping it, to serve the city without losing the Kingdom.

Pastors and leaders can guide this restoration through:

- Teaching eschatological hope – reminding believers that history bends toward resurrection, not ruin.

- Practicing interdependence – partnering across racial and denominational lines to embody the unity Jesus prayed for.

- Cultivating contemplative prayer – silence that dethrones anxiety and attunes hearts to the Shepherd's voice.

- Celebrating sacramental life – baptism and Eucharist as the politics of peace, declaring our primary citizenship in Christ.

When the Church lives this way, her witness becomes luminous again. The world will not confuse her with a party or a platform but recognize in her the fragrance of Christ (2 Corinthians 2:15).

The seduction of nationalism thrives on fear of loss. The restoration of witness begins with love that casts out fear. The Spirit still breathes through weary congregations, whispering what the angel once said to the women at the tomb: "Do not be afraid... He is risen."

That resurrection is the Church's politics. It announces that no empire has the final word. The Shepherd's voice calls His people once more to follow—not into the fortress of nostalgia but onto the open road of mission.

And as they walk, the wind carries a familiar refrain through the trees:

"The Kingdoms of this world have become the Kingdom of our Lord and of His Christ, and He shall reign forever and ever" (Revelation 11:15).

That is the anthem of a restored witness.

Scriptural Anchors

Acts 17:26 – "From one man he made all the nations, that they should inhabit the whole earth." Philippians 3:20 – "But our citizenship is in heaven."

Matthew 6:33 – "But seek first his kingdom and his righteousness, and all these things will be given to you as well."

Reflection Questions

- Which of the seductions of WCN or RCN have you seen most clearly in your community or church? How do these seductions exploit natural longings for belonging, security, purpose, or power?

　
_____

_____

_____

- What historical myths about "Christian America" have you encountered, and how do they shape current debates?

_____

_____

_____

- How do the Scriptures above redirect our attention away from nationalism toward Christ's Kingdom?

- How can you lovingly challenge friends or family members who have been drawn into these seductions?

CHAPTER 13

THE HISTORICAL CONSEQUENCES OF NATIONALISM IN THE CHURCH

Nationalism within the church is not a new phenomenon. History provides sobering examples of what happens when the church aligns itself with worldly power and nationalism. These case studies reveal the destructive fruit of such fusions and provide warnings for today. Each example demonstrates that when faith is co-opted by nationalism or authoritarianism, the gospel is distorted, the church's witness is then compromised, and the name of Christ is dishonored, resulting in significant harm.

The Crusades

In the Middle Ages, the church launched holy wars known as the Crusades. National and religious fervor merged, leading to violence, conquest, and bloodshed in the name of Christ. The Crusades left a legacy of mistrust and devastation that continues to shape Christian-Muslim relations today.

Slavery and Segregation

In America, Christianity was used to justify slavery and, later, segregation. Passages of Scripture were twisted to defend racial hierarchy and oppression. Churches often stood silent—or complicit—while injustice was baptized in religious language. This fusion of faith and racism still casts a long shadow.

Nazi Germany

In the 20th century, many German churches aligned themselves with Adolf Hitler and the Nazi regime. Nationalism fused with distorted Christianity to support policies of anti-Semitism, conquest, and genocide. While some resisted, too many remained silent or supportive, enabling great evil.

Cult Tragedies

In more recent decades, groups such as the People's Temple under Jim Jones and the Branch Davidians under David Koresh demonstrate how distorted faith fused with authoritarian nationalism can lead to death and destruction. In these cases, leaders manipulated followers through fear, false promises, and isolation.

January 6, 2021

The storming of the U.S. Capitol on January 6, 2021, revealed another consequence of nationalism fused with Christian imagery. Prayers were offered "in Jesus' name" while violence and chaos erupted. While not all participants claimed Christian faith, the presence of Christian symbols and language showed how deeply this fusion has influenced American culture.

Scriptural Anchor

Proverbs 14:34: "Righteousness exalts a nation, but sin condemns any people." Nations rise and fall by their righteousness, not by their cultural dominance or political power.

Reflection Questions

- Which of the historical examples (Crusades, slavery/segregation, Nazi Germany, cult tragedies, January 6th) stands out to you most, and why?

_____

_____

_____

- How do these examples show the dangers of aligning faith with nationalism or authoritarian leaders? What lessons can the church learn from these historical consequences today?

_____

_____

_____

CHAPTER 13—*Reflection Questions*

- How does Proverbs 14:34 provide a corrective lens for evaluating nations and movements? How might acknowledging these historical failures strengthen the church's witness today?

_____

_____

_____

CHAPTER 14

THE FRUITS OF NATIONALISM IN THE CHURCH TODAY

The historical consequences of nationalism in the church are sobering, but the danger isn't confined to the past. Even today, the fusion of faith and nationalism bears destructive fruit in Christian communities.

Division

Nationalism divides the body of Christ along political, racial, and cultural lines. Instead of unity in Christ, believers are separated by earthly allegiances. This division weakens the church's witness and fractures relationships.

Fear-Based Discipleship

When nationalism takes root, discipleship often centers on fear of cultural decline, fear of outsiders, and fear of losing influence. Fear replaces love as the motivating force, contrary to 1 John 4:18: "There is no fear in love. But perfect love drives out fear."

Compromised Witness

When churches align too closely with nationalism, the gospel message is compromised. Outsiders see the church not as proclaiming Christ, but as defending power and privilege. This confuses the church's mission and can deter many from the faith.

Idolatry of Power

Nationalism tempts believers to idolize political leaders or systems. Instead of trusting Christ, they put their hope in earthly rulers. Jeremiah 17:5 warns, "Cursed is the one who trusts in man, who draws strength from mere flesh and whose heart turns away from the Lord."

Hollow Discipleship

Where nationalism dominates, discipleship is reduced to political loyalty rather than spiritual transformation. Believers may be passionate about defending cultural values, but lack depth in prayer, Scripture, and Christ-like living.

The Alternative: Kingdom Fruit

Against this destructive fruit, Jesus reminds us of the Kingdom's fruit:

- Unity across dividing lines (Galatians 3:28)

- Love as the foundation of discipleship (John 13:35)
- A witness centered on Christ alone (1 Corinthians 2:2)
- Trust in God rather than human power (Psalm 20:7)

Reflection Questions

- Which of the destructive fruits of nationalism (division, fear, compromised witness, idolatry of power, hollow discipleship) have you seen most clearly in the church today?

  _____

  _____

  _____

- How do these fruits contrast with the fruit of the Spirit and the Kingdom of God?

  _____

  _____

  _____

- What role does fear play in shaping discipleship under nationalism? How does perfect love challenge this fear?

  _____

  _____

  _____

CHAPTER 14—*Reflection Questions*

- How might a compromised witness be repaired or restored in communities affected by nationalism?

  _____

  _____

  _____

- What practices can help cultivate Kingdom fruit in your own life and community?

  _____

  _____

  _____

PART 4

THE WAY FORWARD

CHAPTER 15

THE BIBLICAL RESPONSE TO NATIONALISM

The challenges of nationalism are real and pressing, but Scripture provides a way forward. The Bible offers wisdom for how believers can respond faithfully, keeping Christ at the center.

Our Citizenship in Heaven

Earthly nations are temporary, but our true citizenship is eternal. This perspective frees us from idolizing any earthly power. Philippians 3:20 reminds us, "But our citizenship is in heaven. And we eagerly await a Savior from there, the Lord Jesus Christ."

Rejecting Idols

Nationalism tempts us to idolize race, culture, or political power. Yet 1 John 5:21 warns, "Dear children, keep yourselves from idols." To follow Christ faithfully, we must reject every rival loyalty that competes with Him. Idolatry isn't just about golden calves or statues; it can be far more subtle. An idol is anything we give our ultimate loyalty, trust, or devotion to, or anything we place at the center of our identity besides Christ.

Recognizing Subtle Idolatry

Idols don't always appear obvious. Sometimes they look like good things, like family, work, ministry, politics, or even leaders we admire. They become idols when they take God's rightful place in our lives.

Practical questions for self-reflection:

- What do I turn to first for security or comfort when I'm anxious?
- Whose approval matters most to me?
- Do I spend more time defending a leader, cause, or opinion than I do defending Christ's truth?
- What do I fear losing the most?

If the answer to any of these questions points to something other than God, it may reveal an idol.

Triggers That Lead to Idolatry

- Fear of loss – clinging to a leader or cause to feel secure

- Desire for belonging – idolizing a group or community to avoid rejection
- Longing for purpose – idolizing work, ministry, or movements that make us feel important
- Admiration – respecting someone shifts into blind loyalty or unquestioned devotion. Even influencers, pastors, or politicians can unintentionally become idols if we stop evaluating their words against Scripture.

Biblical Guidance for Guarding Against Idolatry

1. Test every spirit (1 John 4:1): Weigh teachings, leaders and even your own desires against God's Word.

2. Set your heart on things above (Colossians 3:2): Regularly re-center your thoughts on Christ, not earthly things.

3. Remember the first commandment (Exodus 20:3): "You shall have no other gods before me." Idolatry begins when anything rivals Him.

4. Stay in community (Hebrews 10:24–25): Trusted brothers and sisters can help us see blind spots when our admiration becomes unhealthy devotion.

5. Pray for awareness (Psalm 139:23–24): Ask God to reveal what quietly competes for your heart.

The Call to Freedom

Rejecting idols isn't about shame; it's about freedom. Idols over-promise and under-deliver, but Christ alone satisfies. By identifying and surrendering what has taken His place, we experience deeper peace, joy, and security.

Unity in Diversity

Revelation 7:9 paints a picture of a great multitude from every nation, tribe, and people worshipping before the throne. The church must reflect this unity in diversity, refusing to be divided by nationalism or cultural pride.

Replacing Fear with Trust

Nationalism often thrives on fear, but Psalm 56:3 teaches us, "When I am afraid, I put my trust in you." Trust in God counters fear-driven narratives and reminds us that He is our refuge.

Serving Rather than Dominating

Jesus redefined greatness: "The greatest among you will be your servant" (Matthew 23:11). The church must resist the temptation to seek dominance and instead embrace servanthood as the path of Christ.

Speaking the Truth in Love

Ephesians 4:15 calls us to "speak the truth in love." Our response to nationalism must be both truthful and loving. We must be firm in conviction, yet gentle in spirit. Truth without love wounds, and love without truth compromises. Together, they reflect Christ.

Reflection Questions

- How does remembering your heavenly citizenship change how you view your earthly nation?

- What idols of race, culture, or politics tempt you most? How can you resist them?

- How can your church more fully reflect the unity in diversity pictured in Revelation 7:9?

CHAPTER 15—*Reflection Questions*

- What fears have you seen nationalism exploit, and how can trust in God counter them?

- What would it look like for you to embrace servanthood rather than seeking influence or dominance?

CHAPTER 16

PRACTICAL TOOLS FOR DISCERNMENT IN DAILY LIFE

*D*iscernment isn't only for leaders or moments of crisis. It's a daily practice, available to every believer. God equips us with practical tools to navigate the noise of life and remain anchored in His truth.

The Scripture Anchor

Psalm 119:105 says, "Your word is a lamp for my feet, a light on my path." Regular engagement with Scripture trains our minds and hearts to recognize God's voice amid competing messages.

The Fruit Test

Jesus said in Matthew 7:16, "By their fruit you will recognize them." The fruit of a teacher, leader, or movement reveals its source. Does it produce love, joy, peace, patience, kindness, goodness, faithfulness, gentleness, and self-control (Galatians 5:22–23)? Or does it produce fear, confusion, and division?

The Community Check

Discernment isn't meant to be practiced alone. Trusted brothers and sisters in Christ can help us test what we sense. Proverbs 11:14 reminds us, "For lack of guidance a nation falls, but victory is won through many advisers."

The Peace Gauge

Colossians 3:15 says, "Let the peace of Christ rule in your hearts." God's Spirit often guides us through peace. If anxiety, coercion, or confusion dominate, it's worth pausing and testing what spirit is at work.

The Humility Mirror

Discernment requires humility. Approaching discernment with humility keeps us teachable and guards us from pride. As 1 Corinthians 8:2 says, "Those who think they know something do not yet know as they ought to know."

The Courage Step

James 1:22 calls us to be "doers of the word, and not hearers only." Discernment without action is incomplete. When God makes His truth clear, courage is needed to live it out.

The Daily Prayer

Finally, discernment grows in prayer. As modeled in Psalm 139:23-24, "Search me, God, and know my heart; test me and know my anxious thoughts. See if there is any offensive way in me, and lead me in the way everlasting."

Reflection Questions

- Which of the tools (Scripture anchor, fruit test, community check, peace gauge, humility mirror, courage step, or daily prayer) do you already practice regularly?

  _____

  _____

  _____

- Which tool challenges you the most, and why?

  _____

  _____

  _____

- How might practicing discernment in daily, small ways prepare you for larger challenges?

  _____

  _____

  _____

CHAPTER 16—*Reflection Questions*

- Who are the trusted advisers you can lean on for discernment? How can you build deeper accountability with them?

  _____

  _____

  _____

- How does prayer shape your ability to discern clearly?

  _____

  _____

  _____

CONCLUSION
Walking Forward in Truth and Love

As we come to the end of this journey, the challenge of discernment remains both urgent and hopeful. We live in a world filled with manipulation, half-truths, and the seductions of nationalism, but God hasn't left us unequipped. He has given us His Word, His Spirit, and His people to guide us.

The Call to Faithfulness

Discernment isn't about fear, suspicion, or endless anxiety. It's about remaining close to Christ, anchored in His Word, and attentive to His Spirit. Our task is to listen, to follow, and to trust. As Jesus said in John 10:27, "My sheep listen to my voice; I know them, and they follow me."

The Cost and the Reward

There will be moments when discernment requires courage, when speaking truth brings risk, and when standing apart feels lonely. Yet the reward is freedom, clarity, and the joy of walking in step with Christ. Galatians 5:1 declares, "It is for freedom that Christ has set us free."

The Way of Love

Above all, discernment must be guided by love. Love for God, love for His truth, and love for people—even those caught in deception. Discernment without love becomes harsh; love without discernment becomes blind. Together, they reflect the way of Christ. As 1 Corinthians 16:14 instructs us, "Do everything in love."

Looking Ahead

The challenges of manipulation and nationalism won't disappear overnight, but neither will God's promises. The church is called to shine as light in the darkness, to live as a community of truth and love, and to bear witness to the Kingdom that cannot be shaken. May we walk forward with courage, clarity, and compassion, always listening for the Shepherd's voice and following Him wherever He leads.

Reflection Questions

- As you look back on this book, what themes stand out to you most?

  _____

  _____

  _____

- Where do you feel most challenged to grow in discernment?

  _____

  _____

  _____

- What gives you hope as you seek to follow Christ faithfully in a noisy world?

  _____

  _____

  _____

- How can your community encourage one another in discernment and love?

- What first step will you take to walk forward in truth and love this week?

APPENDICES INTRODUCTION

The following appendices are provided as study tools to help deepen your understanding and application of the lessons in this book. Each section offers a way to engage with the book's message through Scripture, reflection, and practical discernment. Use these resources for personal growth, small group discussion, or teaching as you continue learning to hear and follow the Shepherd's voice.

APPENDIX A
SCRIPTURE REFERENCES

Holy Bible, New International Version®, NIV® Copyright ©1973, 1978, 1984, 2011 by Biblica, Inc.® Used by permission. All rights reserved worldwide.

Part I: Foundations of Discernment

CHAPTER 1 – *The Fork in the Road*

Genesis 1:3 – God speaks creation into being.

Colossians 4:6 – Let your conversation be full of grace.

Ephesians 4:25 – Speak truthfully to your neighbor.

1 Corinthians 13:1 – Without love, words are meaningless noise.

James 1:19 – Be quick to listen, slow to speak.

John 10:10 – Jesus gives life abundantly; the thief destroys.

CHAPTER 2 – *The Anatomy of Manipulation*

2 Corinthians 11:14–15 – Satan masquerades as an angel of light.

Ephesians 5:11 – Expose the fruitless deeds of darkness.

CHAPTER 3 – *The Wolf in Shepherd's Clothing*

1 Samuel 2:12–17 – Eli's sons abuse their priestly power.

Matthew 23:23–24 – Pharisees neglect justice and mercy.

Acts 8:9–23 – Simon the sorcerer seeks spiritual power for gain.

Matthew 7:15 – Beware of false prophets in sheep's clothing.

Numbers 16 – Korah's rebellion was misused as a control tactic.

Proverbs 6:16–19 – Seven things the Lord hates.

James 4:6 – God opposes the proud but gives grace to the humble.

John 8:44 – Satan is the father of lies.

Genesis 4:10 – Abel's blood cries out from the ground.

Jeremiah 17:9 – The heart is deceitful above all things.

Isaiah 59:7 – Feet run to evil and shed innocent blood.

Exodus 20:16 – Do not bear false witness.

Psalm 133:1 – How good and pleasant it is when God's people live in unity.

APPENDIX A—*Scripture References*

Malachi 2:16 – God hates unfaithfulness.

Zechariah 8:17 – He hates false oaths and evil plans.

Amos 5:21–23 – God rejects worship without justice.

1 John 4:1 – Test the spirits.

CHAPTER 4 – *The Biblical Foundation of Discernment*

Romans 12:2 – Be transformed by the renewing of your mind.

Hebrews 5:14 – Train to distinguish good from evil.

1 Thessalonians 5:21 – Test everything; hold to the good.

Philippians 4:7 – Peace of God guards hearts and minds.

Galatians 6:1 – Restore gently those caught in sin.

Part II: Everyday Responses

CHAPTER 5 – *Navigating Voices and Opinions*

2 Corinthians 10:5 – Take every thought captive to Christ.

John 14:6 – Jesus is the way, the truth, and the life.

CHAPTER 6 – *The Fruits of Manipulation*

Matthew 7:16 – By their fruit you will recognize them.

1 Corinthians 14:33 – God is not a God of disorder but of peace.

1 John 4:18 – Perfect love drives out fear.

Romans 8:1 – No condemnation for those in Christ.

John 17:21 – Jesus prays for unity among believers.

Matthew 11:28 – Come to Me, and I will give you rest.

Galatians 5:22–23 – The fruit of the Spirit.

CHAPTER 7 – *The Cost of Silence*

James 4:17 – Knowing the good and not doing it is sin.

Proverbs 31:8–9 – Speak up for the voiceless and the poor.

Ezekiel 33:7–8 – The watchman's responsibility to warn.

Matthew 23 – Jesus rebukes leaders who distort truth.

Galatians 2:11–14 – Paul confronts Peter for hypocrisy.

Part III: The Cultural Challenge of Nationalism

CHAPTER 8 – *The Unsettling Fusion*

1 Samuel 8:5 – Israel demands a king.

Acts 5:29 – Obey God rather than men.

Psalm 146:3 – Do not put trust in princes.

APPENDIX A—*Scripture References*

CHAPTER 9 – *White Christian Nationalism*
   John 18:36 – My kingdom is not of this world.
   Galatians 3:28 – All are one in Christ Jesus.
   Philippians 3:20 – Our citizenship is in heaven.
   Acts 10:34–35 – God shows no favoritism.
   1 Samuel 8:10–18 – Warning of oppressive kingship.
   Mark 12:17 – Render to Caesar what is Caesar's.
   Hebrews 11:13–16 – God's people seek a better country.
   Luke 13:29 – People come from all nations into the kingdom.
   Ephesians 1:4–6 – Election in Christ.
   Matthew 28:19–20 – The Great Commission to all nations.
   1 Corinthians 1:12–13 – Condemnation of division.
   Psalm 33:12 – Blessed is the nation whose God is the Lord.
   Micah 6:8 – Do justice, love mercy, walk humbly.
   Revelation 7:9 – Every tribe and tongue before the Lamb.
   1 John 4:18 – Perfect love casts out fear.
   Philippians 2:7 – Christ took the nature of a servant.

CHAPTER 10 – *Right-Wing Christian Nationalism*
   Isaiah 5:20 – Woe to those who call evil good.
   Matthew 23:23 – Neglecting justice and mercy.

1 John 4:18 – Fear replaced by love.

Revelation 13 (implied) – Beast imagery as critique of empire.

2 Corinthians 12:9 – God's power made perfect in weakness.

Matthew 4:8–10 – Jesus rejects worldly kingdoms.

2 Samuel 12:1–7 – Nathan confronts David.

Amos 5:21–24 – God rejects worship without justice.

2 Timothy 2:24 – The Lord's servant must be kind to all.

Galatians 5:22–23 – Fruit of the Spirit.

Matthew 5:13 – Salt losing distinctiveness.

Romans 13:1–7 – Respect for governing authorities.

Acts 5:29 – Obey God rather than men.

Matthew 5:3–10 – The Beatitudes.

CHAPTER 11 – *The Seduction of Nationalism*

Psalm 137:1–6 – Longing for homeland.

Revelation 21:1–5 – New heaven and new earth.

1 John 4:18 – Perfect love casts out fear.

John 18:36 – Kingdom not of this world.

Genesis 3:5 – "You will be like God."

Isaiah 30:15 – In quietness and trust is your strength.

John 13:3–15 – Jesus washes the disciples' feet.

John 1:14 – The Word became flesh.

Philippians 2:6–8 – Christ humbled Himself.

Matthew 28:19–20 – Make disciples of all nations.

John 13:35 – Known by love.

John 6:20 – "It is I; do not be afraid."

Jeremiah 29:7 – Seek the peace of the city.

Hebrews 12:28 – A kingdom that cannot be shaken.

CHAPTER 12 – *Restoring the Witness*

Matthew 5:14 – You are the light of the world.

Genesis 12:3 – All families of the earth are blessed.

Deuteronomy 10:19 – Love the stranger.

2 Corinthians 12:9 – Power in weakness.

Acts 2 – Spirit unites languages.

Hebrews 13:2 – Some have entertained angels unawares.

Revelation 5:6 – The Lamb on the throne.

1 John 1:9 – Confess sins for cleansing.

1 Peter 2:9 – A chosen people, a holy nation.

Revelation 7:9 – Every tribe and tongue before the Lamb.

Hebrews 11:10 – City whose builder is God.

John 17:14–18 – In the world but not of it.

2 Corinthians 2:15 – The fragrance of Christ.

Revelation 11:15 – The kingdoms of this world become Christ's.

Psalm 33:12 – Blessed is the nation whose God is the Lord.

Matthew 6:33 – Seek first the Kingdom.

CHAPTER 13 – *Historical Consequences*

Proverbs 14:34 – Righteousness exalts a nation.

CHAPTER 14 – *Fruits of Nationalism in the Church Today*

1 John 4:18 – Perfect love drives out fear.

Jeremiah 17:5 – Cursed is the one who trusts in man.

Galatians 3:28 – Unity in Christ.

John 13:35 – Love one another.

1 Corinthians 2:2 – Christ and Him crucified.

Psalm 20:7 – We trust in the name of the Lord.

Part IV: The Way Forward

CHAPTER 15 – *The Biblical Response to Nationalism*

Philippians 3:20 – Citizenship in heaven.

1 John 5:21 – Keep yourselves from idols.

1 John 4:1 – Test the spirits.

Colossians 3:2 – Set your minds on things above.

Exodus 20:3 – No other gods before Me.

APPENDIX A—*Scripture References*

Hebrews 10:24–25 – Do not neglect meeting together.

Psalm 139:23–24 – Search me, O God.

Revelation 7:9 – Unity in diversity.

Psalm 56:3 – When I am afraid, I trust in You.

Matthew 23:11 – The greatest will be your servant.

Ephesians 4:15 – Speak the truth in love.

CHAPTER 16 – *Practical Tools for Discernment in Daily Life*

Psalm 119:105 – Your word is a lamp to my feet.

Matthew 7:16 – By their fruit you will know them.

Galatians 5:22–23 – Fruit of the Spirit.

Proverbs 11:14 – Victory through many advisers.

Colossians 3:15 – Let the peace of Christ rule in your hearts.

1 Corinthians 8:2 – We do not yet know as we ought.

James 1:22 – Be doers of the Word.

Psalm 139:23–24 – Search me, O God.

CONCLUSION – *Walking Forward in Truth and Love*

John 10:27 – My sheep listen to My voice.

Galatians 5:1 – For freedom Christ has set us free.

1 Corinthians 16:14 – Do everything in love.

John 17:14–18 – In the world but not of it.

Study Cross-Reference Table *(Themes & Tie-Ins)*

THEME / TOPIC	KEY SCRIPTURES	TIE-IN PASSAGES
Manipulation & Deception	2 Corinthians 11:14–15; Matthew 7:15; Ephesians 5:11	2 Peter 2:1–3; Jeremiah 23:1–2
Discernment & Truth	Romans 12:2; Hebrews 5:14; 1 Thessalonians 5:21	1 John 4:1; Psalm 119:105
Weaponized Faith	Matthew 23:23–24; 1 Samuel 2:12–17	John 8:44; Proverbs 6:16–19
Fear vs. Love	1 John 4:18; Psalm 56:3	Philippians 4:7; 2 Timothy 1:7
Faith & Politics	1 Samuel 8:5; Acts 5:29; Psalm 146:3	John 18:36; Mark 12:17
Nationalism & Idolatry	Philippians 3:20; Revelation 7:9; Jeremiah 17:5	Matthew 6:33; Micah 6:8
Unity & Kingdom Witness	John 17:21; 1 Cor. 1:12–13	Eph. 4:15; Gal. 3:28
Fruit of the Spirit	Galatians 5:22–23; Matthew 7:16	John 15:5; Romans 8:1

APPENDIX B

REFLECTION & DISCUSSION GUIDE

Part I: Foundations of Discernment

CHAPTER 1 – *The Fork in the Road:*
Two Paths of Communication

- How does understanding communication as a spiritual act change the way we speak and listen daily?

_____

- Where have you seen words used to build trust—or destroy it—in your family, church, or workplace?

- What practical habits can help ensure your speech aligns with truth, clarity, and love?

_____

_____

_____

CHAPTER 2 – *The Anatomy of Manipulation*

- Which manipulation tactics (emotional exploitation, gaslighting, spiritualizing, withholding) do you recognize most in your environment?

_____

_____

_____

- Why do you think manipulation often appears "helpful" at first?

_____

_____

_____

- How can you create healthy boundaries that expose manipulation without returning harm for harm?

CHAPTER 3 – *The Wolf in Shepherd's Clothing*
- What are some warning signs that faith or leadership is being used for control rather than care?

- How can believers distinguish between conviction that leads to repentance and fear that leads to bondage?

- In what ways can spiritual accountability protect communities from religious abuse?

_____

_____

_____

CHAPTER 4 – *The Biblical Foundation of Discernment*
- How does Scripture define discernment differently from suspicion or judgment?

_____

_____

_____

- What role does peace play in confirming that discernment is from God?

_____

_____

_____

- Who can you invite into your life to help test your discernment with wisdom and grace?

Part II: Everyday Responses

CHAPTER 5 – *"It's Just a Difference of Opinion"*

- Why do opinions matter spiritually, not just socially or politically?

- How can believers practice discernment when engaging with influencers or online debates?

- What's the difference between holding strong convictions and being closed to correction?

CHAPTER 6 – *The Fruits of Manipulation*
- Which "fruit" of manipulation—confusion, fear, shame, or division—have you witnessed most often in the church?

- How do these fruits contrast with the fruit of the Spirit in Galatians 5?

- What personal practices help you stay grounded in peace when manipulation surrounds you?

CHAPTER 7 – *The Cost of Silence*
- What keeps people silent in the face of wrongdoing—fear, comfort, or lack of confidence?

- How can silence harm both individuals and the witness of the Church?

- What are small, faithful ways to speak up with courage and love?

Part III: The Cultural Challenge of Nationalism

CHAPTER 8 – *The Unsettling Fusion*

- How has the blending of faith and politics changed the public's view of Christianity?

- What does the story of Israel's demand for a king teach us about trusting human power?

- How can the church stay engaged in culture without losing its prophetic voice?

CHAPTER 9 – *What Is White Christian Nationalism?*
- Why does fusing racial identity with divine favor contradict the gospel?

- How can the Church address this distortion without alienating those caught in it?

- In what ways does remembering the global, multiethnic body of Christ correct nationalistic thinking?

_____

_____

_____

CHAPTER 10 – *What Is Right-Wing Christian Nationalism?*
- How does RCN differ from genuine political engagement guided by faith?

_____

_____

_____

- Why is it dangerous when partisan loyalty replaces loyalty to Christ?

_____

_____

_____

- What spiritual disciplines can help keep our focus on Kingdom values instead of culture wars?

CHAPTER 11 – *The Seduction of Nationalism*
- Why is nationalism emotionally appealing to many believers?

- How can longing for belonging or fear of loss lead to misplaced devotion?

- What Scriptures remind you that our true home and security are found in Christ?

CHAPTER 12 – *Restoring the Witness*
- What does it mean to be "a city on a hill" in today's divided world?

- How can humility and hospitality rebuild the Church's credibility?

- What steps can your community take to embody Christ's love across political or cultural lines?

CHAPTER 13 – *Historical Consequences*
- Which historical examples most clearly show how nationalism corrupts faith?

- How can learning from history protect the modern Church from repeating these errors?

- What does Proverbs 14:34 teach us about true national righteousness?

_____

_____

_____

CHAPTER 14 – *Fruits of Nationalism in the Church Today*
- Which fruits of nationalism—division, fear, idolatry, hollow discipleship—do you see most clearly today?

_____

_____

_____

- How can churches reclaim a Christ-centered identity that unites rather than divides?

_____

_____

_____

- What does "trusting in the Lord instead of princes" look like in daily discipleship?

Part IV: The Way Forward

CHAPTER 15 – *The Biblical Response to Nationalism*

- What idols subtly compete for your devotion besides Christ?

- How does remembering heavenly citizenship reshape your identity and priorities?

- How can churches cultivate unity in diversity as pictured in Revelation 7:9?

_____

_____

_____

CHAPTER 16 – *Practical Tools for Discernment*
- Which discernment tools (Scripture anchor, peace gauge, community check, etc.) do you need to strengthen most?

_____

_____

_____

- How can you practice discernment in ordinary moments—conversations, media, leadership, relationships?

_____

_____

_____

- Who are your trusted voices of accountability, and how can you deepen that partnership?

CONCLUSION – *Walking Forward in Truth and Love*
- How do truth and love balance each other in discernment?

- What personal change do you feel called to make after studying this material?

- How can your group continue growing together in discernment beyond this book?

APPENDIX C
KEY TERMS & DEFINITIONS

Discernment
Definition: The Spirit-led ability to distinguish between truth and deception.

Biblical Context: Hebrews 5:14 – 'Solid food is for the mature, who by constant use have trained themselves to distinguish good from evil.'

Proof-Texting
Definition: The misuse of Scripture by quoting verses out of context to support a personal or political agenda.

Biblical Context: 2 Timothy 2:15 – 'Do your best to present yourself to God as one approved… who correctly handles the word of truth.'

Christian Nationalism
Definition: A belief system that merges national identity and political ideology with Christianity in ways that distort the gospel's message of unity and grace.

Biblical Context: Galatians 3:28 – 'All are one in Christ Jesus.'

REFERENCES

The Holy Bible, *New International Version* (NIV). Grand Rapids: Zondervan, 2011. (*Unless otherwise noted, all Scripture quotations are taken from the NIV translation.*)

Bauckham, R. (1993). *The theology of the Book of Revelation.* Cambridge University Press.

Bellah, R. N. (1967). Civil religion in America. *Daedalus, 96*(1), 1–21.

Brooks, D. (2019). *The second mountain: The quest for a moral life.* Random House.

Butler, C. (2021). *White evangelical racism: The politics of morality in America.* University of North Carolina Press.

De Gruchy, J. W. (1986). *The church struggle in South Africa.* Eerdmans.

Du Mez, K. K. (2020). *Jesus and John Wayne: How white evangelicals corrupted a faith and fractured a nation.* Liveright.

Emerson, M. O., & Smith, C. (2000). *Divided by faith: Evangelical religion and the problem of race in America.* Oxford University Press.

Fea, J. (2018). *Believe me: The evangelical road to Donald Trump.* Eerdmans.

Galli, M. (2019, December 20). The spiritual danger of political idolatry. Christianity Today. https://www.christianitytoday.com

Gorski, P. S. (2017). *American covenant: A history of civil religion from the Puritans to the present*. Princeton University Press.

Gorski, P. S., & Perry, S. L. (2022). *The flag and the cross: White Christian nationalism and the threat to American democracy*. Oxford University Press.

Herzog, J. (2010). *The spiritual-industrial complex: America's religious battle against communism in the early Cold War*. Oxford University Press.

Horsman, R. (1981). *Race and manifest destiny: The origins of American racial Anglo-Saxonism*. Harvard University Press.

Jenkins, P. (2011). *The next Christendom: The coming of global Christianity* (3rd ed.). Oxford University Press.

Jones, R. P. (2016). *The end of white Christian America*. Simon & Schuster.

Marsden, G. M. (2006). *Fundamentalism and American culture* (2nd ed.). Oxford University Press.

McCracken, B. (2021). *The wisdom pyramid: Feeding your soul in a post-truth world*. Crossway.

Moltmann, J. (1972). *The theology of hope*. Harper & Row.

Noll, M. A. (2002). *America's God: From Jonathan Edwards to Abraham Lincoln*. Oxford University Press.

Perry, S. L., & Gorski, P. S. (2022). *The flag and the cross: White Christian nationalism and the threat to American democracy*. Oxford University Press. [Duplicate of Gorski & Perry (2022); keep one entry only—see above.]

Perry, S. L., & Whitehead, A. L. (2020). *Taking America back for God: Christian nationalism in the United States*. Oxford University Press.

Putnam, R. D. (2020). *The upswing: How America came together—and how we can do it again*. Simon & Schuster.

Stewart, K. (2021). *The power worshippers: Inside the dangerous rise of religious nationalism.* Bloomsbury.

Whitehead, A. L. (2021). Christian nationalism and the future of faith. Sociology of Religion, 82(4), 411–429. https://doi.org/10.1093/socrel/srab030

Whitehead, A. L., & Perry, S. L. (2020). *Taking America back for God: Christian nationalism in the United States.* Oxford University Press. [Retained single instance.]

Wright, N. T. (2012). How God became King: *The forgotten story of the Gospels.* HarperOne.

Slavery and Segregation in America (17th–20th centuries) Nazi Germany and the Holocaust (1933–1945)

Jim Jones and The People's Temple (1970s), David Koresh and the Branch Davidians (1993)

Robert Shinn and Shekinah Church (1990s–present) January 6, 2021 – U.S. Capitol riot

The Moral Majority and Religious Right movements (late 20th century)

ABOUT THE AUTHOR

*W*hile many creatives are focused on their goals, aspirations, and dreams, he's committed to ensuring that every one of his creative gifts points people back to God. As an educator, media professional, and creative leader, Tonnines Elliott is best known for helping business owners worldwide build online platforms that reflect both excellence and integrity. With more than twenty years of experience in communication, design, and ministry experience, he proudly serves as the founder and Creative Services Director of Melting Pot Media Inc., spearheading design, e-commerce, and digital marketing projects for businesses and ministries across the country. A U.S. Air Force veteran who served honorably during Desert Storm and Desert Shield, Tonnines has carried his passion for service and discipline into every area of his professional and creative life, setting him apart from most competitors.

Holding a Master of Science in Education, Media Design and Technology from Full Sail University, as well as a Bachelor of Science in Business Administration from the

University of Phoenix, Tonnines served as an adjunct professor at the International Academy of Design and Technology, where he was recognized for his engaging teaching and mentorship. In addition to his work being featured in the school's publication *IADT Detroit Spotlight*, he was also able to launch *BSocial Magazine*, where he collaborated with local artists, well-known actors, musicians, fashion designers, publicists, and writers. Under his direction, the publication achieved a readership of over 100,000, giving him firsthand experience in creating content that connects with large, globally diverse audiences.

In his debut book, *The Shepherd's Voice: A Journey of Discernment in a Noisy World,* Tonnines offers a timely, compassionate guide for Christians seeking clarity in an age of deception, distraction and spiritual confusion. Serving as a catalyst to heal parishioners who have been deceived, manipulated and abused spiritually for decades, he intentionally shines a light on how the Word has been twisted and tainted in today's North American Church at large. On a mission to end the prominent everyday abuse many suffer in silence with on pews around the nation, Tonnines gives readers an inside scoop on truly hearing the voice of God for themselves so they can live a life of freedom and fulfillment.

ABOUT THE AUTHOR

Proudly serving as Minister of Media at his home church, Tonnines has spent over a decade leading creative teams in live production, digital outreach, and visual storytelling. His life and work truly reflect a unified calling unapologetically. For booking or speaking engagements, email meltingpotmediainc@gmail.com.

www.ingramcontent.com/pod-product-compliance
Lightning Source LLC
LaVergne TN
LVHW021237080526
838199LV00088B/4554